UNITED STATES
HOLY GROUND
★ ★ ★ ★ ★
GUIDEBOOK

The Family Federation for World Peace and Unification, USA

Copyright © 2017 by the Family Federation
for World Peace and Unification

Published by The Holy Spirit Association
for the Unification of World Christianity (HSA-UWC)

HSA-UWC
4 West 43rd Street, New York, NY 10036

ISBN: 978-1-931166-66-9

All rights reserved. No part of this publication may be reproduced, stored in a retrieval system or transmitted, in any form, or by any means, electronic, mechanical, recorded, photocopied, or otherwise, without the prior written permission of both the copyright owner and the above publisher of this book, except by a reviewer who may quote brief passages in a review.

The scanning, uploading, and distribution of this book via the Internet or via any other means without the permission of the publisher is illegal and punishable by law. Please purchase only authorized electronic editions and do not participate in or encourage electronic piracy of copyrightable materials. Your support of the author's rights is appreciated.

Printed in the United States of America

GOD'S HOPE for AMERICA.org

43 DAYS
55 HOLY GROUNDS

God has been working throughout history to bring about a peaceful world. God's Hope for America is that it fulfill its unique destiny and establish peaceful, God-centered individuals, families, communities and a nation that can lead other nations towards building One World Under God.

"Holy Grounds were made as places to pray. During the difficult times, when we had no place to pray and we were being pushed and persecuted, the selection of the Holy Grounds – where we could express our heart to God – was truly historic. We need to understand that this event planted the seeds of worldwide victory.

"I traveled through the entire United States of America within 40 days. During that time I selected and created Holy Grounds. Because of the special conditions that I made, a Holy Ground is a place where we can possess God's love. The reason why I created more Holy Grounds in the United States than in any other nation was to declare that the final settlement will be brought in this nation. I placed more importance on each U.S. state than on a nation. In other words, I regarded the United States to be the center of the world and the universe.

"If you see the Holy Grounds as the center, the land where you are standing represents 120 Holy Grounds in 40 nations. Since the altar where you are standing represents the entire world, you stand as a representative of the world. Further, when you pray, bowing down, you come to pray as a chief priest in the position of an offering object, asking for the forgiveness of the sins of all humankind."

—Reverend Sun Myung Moon

CONTENTS

Introduction 5
Foreword 7

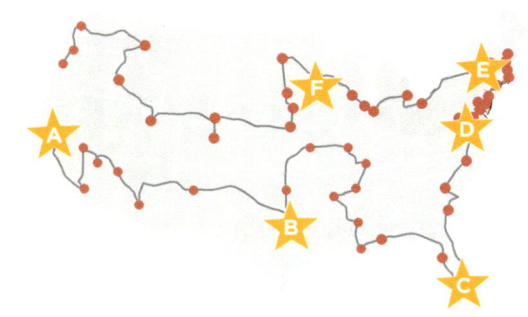

Ⓐ PACIFIC 10
San Francisco, CA 12
Los Angeles, CA 14
Mt. Whitney, CA 16
Death Valley, CA 18
Las Vegas, NV 20
Phoenix, AZ 22
Albuquerque, NM 24

Ⓑ GATEWAY 30
Dallas, TX 32
Oklahoma City, OK 34
Kansas City, KS 36
St. Louis, MO 38
Paducah, KY 40
Memphis, TN 42
Little Rock, AR 44
Jackson, MS 46
New Orleans, LA 48
Mobile, AL 50
Tampa, FL 52
Miami, FL 54
Savannah, GA 56

Ⓒ CAPITAL 60
Columbia, SC 62
Raleigh, NC 64
Richmond, VA 66
Martinsburg, WV 68
Washington, D.C. 70

Ⓓ ATLANTIC 76
Baltimore, MD 78
Wilmington, DE 80
Philadelphia, PA 82
Trenton, NJ 84
New York, NY 86
New Haven, CT 92
Providence, RI 94
Boston, MA 96
Kittery, ME 98
Portsmouth, NH 100
Brattleboro, VT 106

Ⓔ MIDWEST 104
Cleveland, OH 108
Detroit, MI 110
Hammond, IN 112
Chicago, IL 114
Madison, WI 116

Ⓕ MOUNTAINS 120
St. Paul, MN 122
Fargo, ND 124
Sioux Falls, SD 126
Sioux City, IA 128
Omaha, NE 130
Cheyenne, WY 132
Denver, CO 134
Salt Lake City, UT 136
Boise, ID 138
Missoula, MT 140
Seattle, WA 142
Portland, OR 144
Eugene, OR 146

GOD'S HOPE FOR AMERICA

Sun Myung Moon was born a farmer's son in 1920, in what is now North Korea. From an early age, he was intensely aware of the suffering ailing humankind and the ineffectiveness of contemporary religions; he sought to understand the origins of suffering and how it might be resolved. On Easter Sunday in 1935, he had a life-changing spiritual encounter with Jesus who tasked him with building God's kingdom on Earth. After deep reflection, meditation and prayer, the 16-year-old pledged to undertake this overwhelming task.

Rev. Moon devoted himself to studying the Bible and other religious texts, discovering God's own suffering and His longing to be reunited with His children. Through intense prayer and setting of conditions, he grasped the difficult steps that humankind would have to undertake to return to God and establish true peace. By 1945, Rev. Moon had finalized the development of his religious teachings, completing the core text of the Unification Church, the Divine Principle, and began sharing his message.

In February 1965, Rev. Moon embarked on a pilgrimage of the United States, taking the first steps toward planting a religious movement that, by the 1970s, had become one of the best known—and controversial—of all the many new faith communities that developed in the United States during that tumultuous decade. He toured the entire continental United States in just six short weeks, a road trip of 10,000 miles in a bright blue '65 Plymouth Fury station wagon. Visiting up to six states a day, his plan was to visit every state and plant a "Holy Ground," a place for meditation and prayers for peace. In each, he buried a cache of soil and stones from his native Korea, at that time still recovering from the ravages of war and civil conflict, and prayed for the day when all nations and all people would become one.

By the end of the tour, 43 days and three oil changes later, he had come to the realization that if his movement were to have any hope of achieving the lofty goal of the unification of all religions, he would need to move his base of operations to the United States.

In September 2012, the Rev. Moon embarked on his final journey, dying at the age of 92 at his home in the mountains outside Seoul.

2016 marks the 50th year of his work in America. To commemorate his legacy, we release the God's Hope for America tour guide.

What is a Holy Ground?

> "Holy Grounds were made as places to pray. During the difficult times, when we had no place to pray and we were being pushed and persecuted, the selection of the Holy Grounds—where we could express our heart to God—was truly historic. We need to understand that this event planted the seeds of worldwide victory.

> "I traveled through the entire United States of America in 43 days. During that time I selected and created Holy Grounds. Because of the special conditions that I made, a Holy Ground is a place where we can possess God's love. The reason why I created more Holy Grounds in the United States than in any other nation was to declare that the final settlement will be brought in this nation. I placed more importance on each U.S. state than on a nation. In other words, I regarded the United States to be the center of the world and the universe.

"If you see the Holy Grounds as the center, the land where you are standing represents 120 Holy Grounds in 40 nations. Since the altar where you are standing represents the entire world, you stand as a representative of the world. Further, when you pray, bowing down, you come to pray as a chief priest in the position of an offering object, asking for the forgiveness of the sins of all humankind."
—Reverend Sun Myung Moon

In the summer of 2014, fifty Unificationists followed—literally—in Rev. Moon's first footsteps in America, driving the same roads and finding out how the Unification community was holding up to the passage of time. With access to recently discovered archival material, journals, photos and early 8mm film footage, the God's Hope for America tour group documented the first half-century of one of the best-known new religious movements in America.

We hope to remember, revive and reimagine the message that God called on Rev. Moon to bring to this country: America is God's hope. Continue exploring this country through the eyes of the best man I have ever known, and in the process rediscover for yourself God's hope for America.

— Dr. Michael Balcomb, President,
Family Federation for World Peace and Unification, USA

1965 TOUR

This is the original map that Rev. Moon used to tour the United States during his first visit. It shows the route the tour took across the U.S. as he established 55 Holy Grounds with the purpose of reviving God's Hope for America.

The **JOURNAL ENTRIES** *in this book are excerpted from notes of that historic journey.*

2014 TOUR

This map, signed by Dr. Hak Ja Han Moon, shows the route that the God's Hope for America Tour followed during the summer of 2014, as they revisited the 55 Holy Grounds that Rev. Moon created in 1965

PACIFIC & ALL ITS WONDERS

REGION A

TRAVEL TIME: FEBRUARY 19, 1965 - FEBRUARY 28, 1965

The Pacific region tour will take you up to the high peaks of Mt. Whitney and down into the sweltering heat of Death Valley, the lowest point in the United States. Take the chance to visit places loved by Rev. and Mrs. Moon, such as the Grand Canyon, Lake Mead and the Hoover Dam.

"It is the time to establish God's throne at the top of the Grand Canyon. People say how the Grand Canyon is great, but there has been no owner who can love it as God does. The Grand Canyon is an amazing creation."

—Rev. Moon, Grand Canyon, January 3, 2011

A PACIFIC

CHECKLIST OF HOLY GROUNDS

- ☐ San Francisco, CA
- ☐ Los Angeles, CA
- ☐ Mt. Whitney, CA
- ☐ Las Vegas, NV
- ☐ Phoenix, AZ
- ☐ Albuquerque, NM

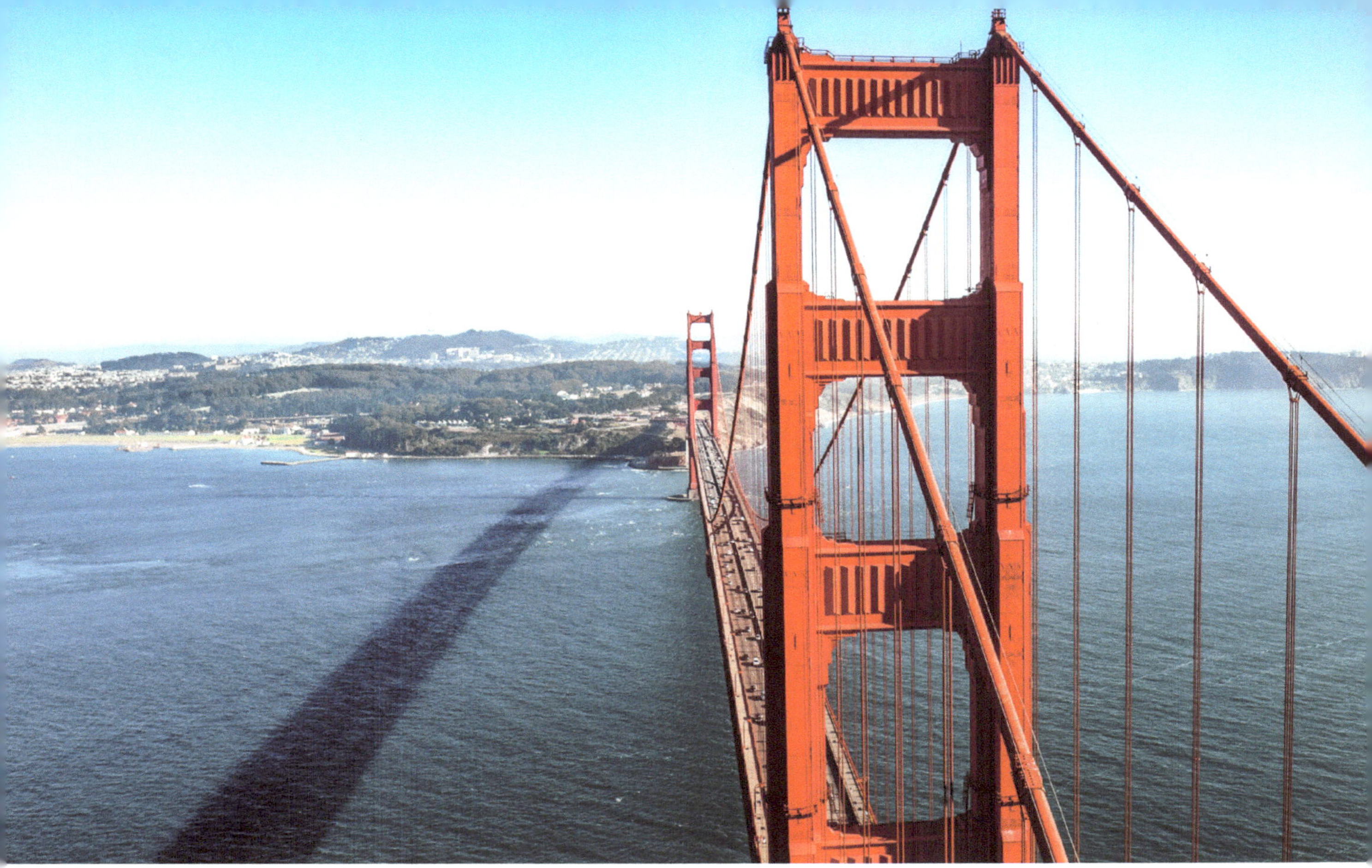

WELCOME
TO Fabulous
LAS VEGAS
NEVADA
GOD'S HOPE for AMERICA
LAS VEGAS, NV
JUNE 29, 2014

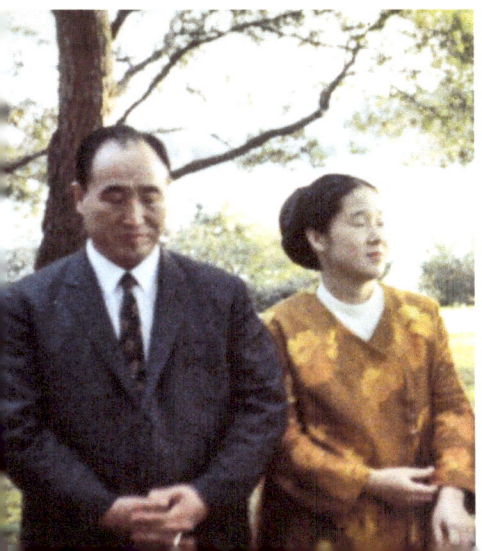

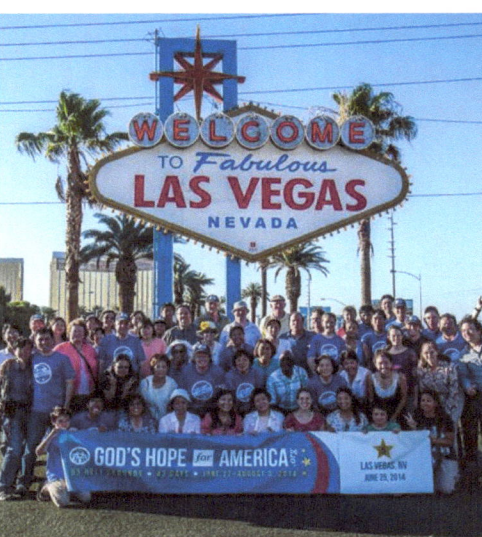

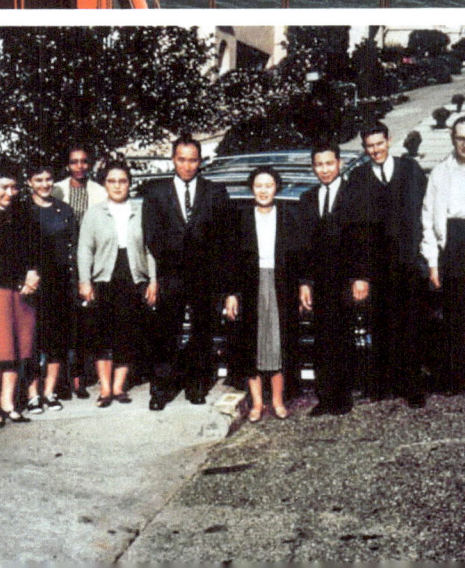

SAN FRANCISCO, CALIFORNIA

HOLY GROUND

EST: FEBRUARY 19, 1965
GPS COORDINATES: 37°45'12.0"N 122°26'50.8"W

LOCATION

The San Francisco Holy Ground sits on Twin Peaks, a large hill in the center of the city. The official location is marked by a rock on top of the northernmost peak, although both peaks are considered to be the Holy Ground. It can get quite windy and cold, so take a sweater just in case.

JOURNAL ENTRY

It was a Sunday evening and Rev. Moon wanted to go up to Twin Peaks in San Francisco to see the lights of the city from the highest place. About 15 people went with him to the top of the peak. Rev. Moon said, "If there is a higher place around, I will climb up to it." He wouldn't be satisfied with anything but the highest spot. As they assembled on the peak overlooking the lights of the city, Rev. Moon stood on a large rock formation and prayed. He told them that night that he would make this spot a Holy Ground, the first of many in the United States.

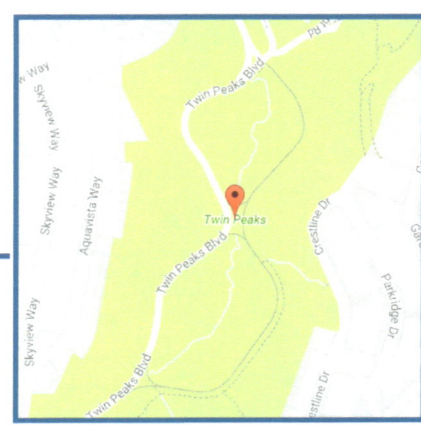

TWIN PEAKS
501 Twin Peaks Blvd,
San Francisco, CA 94114

To Mrs. Moon

After coming to America, and as we remain apart, I realize all the more how precious we are to each other, and what a great mission we share. The feeling that comes with that realization is something I am very grateful for. How crucial is our lifelong duty!

-Rev. Moon, February 15, 1965, San Francisco, CA

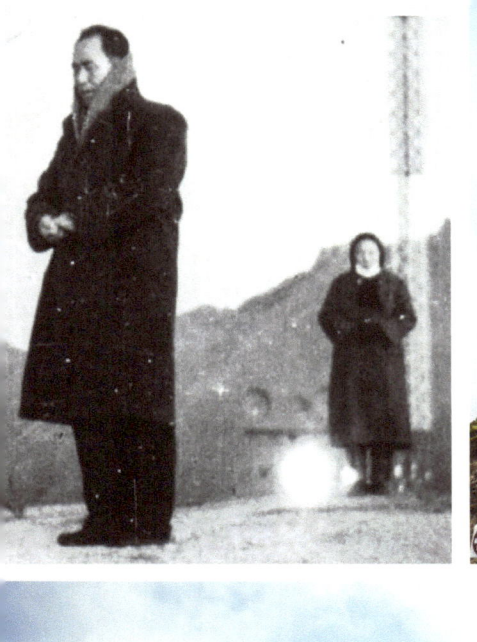

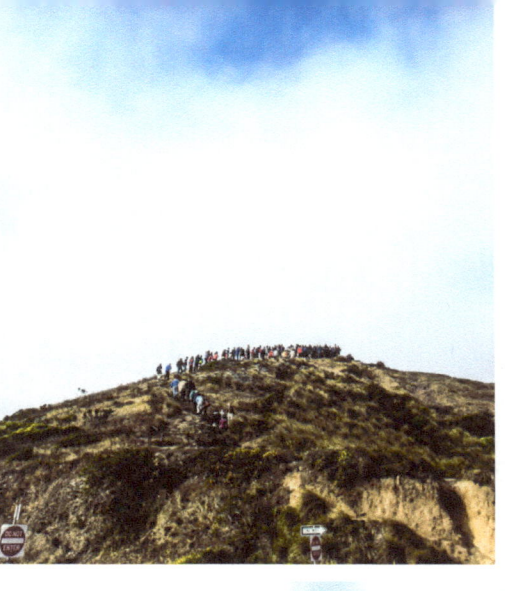

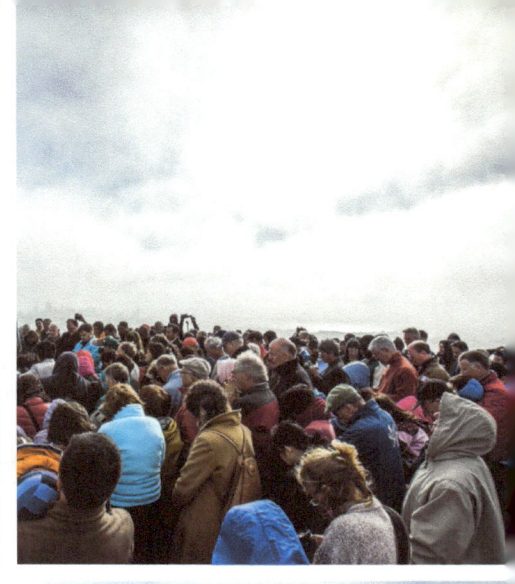

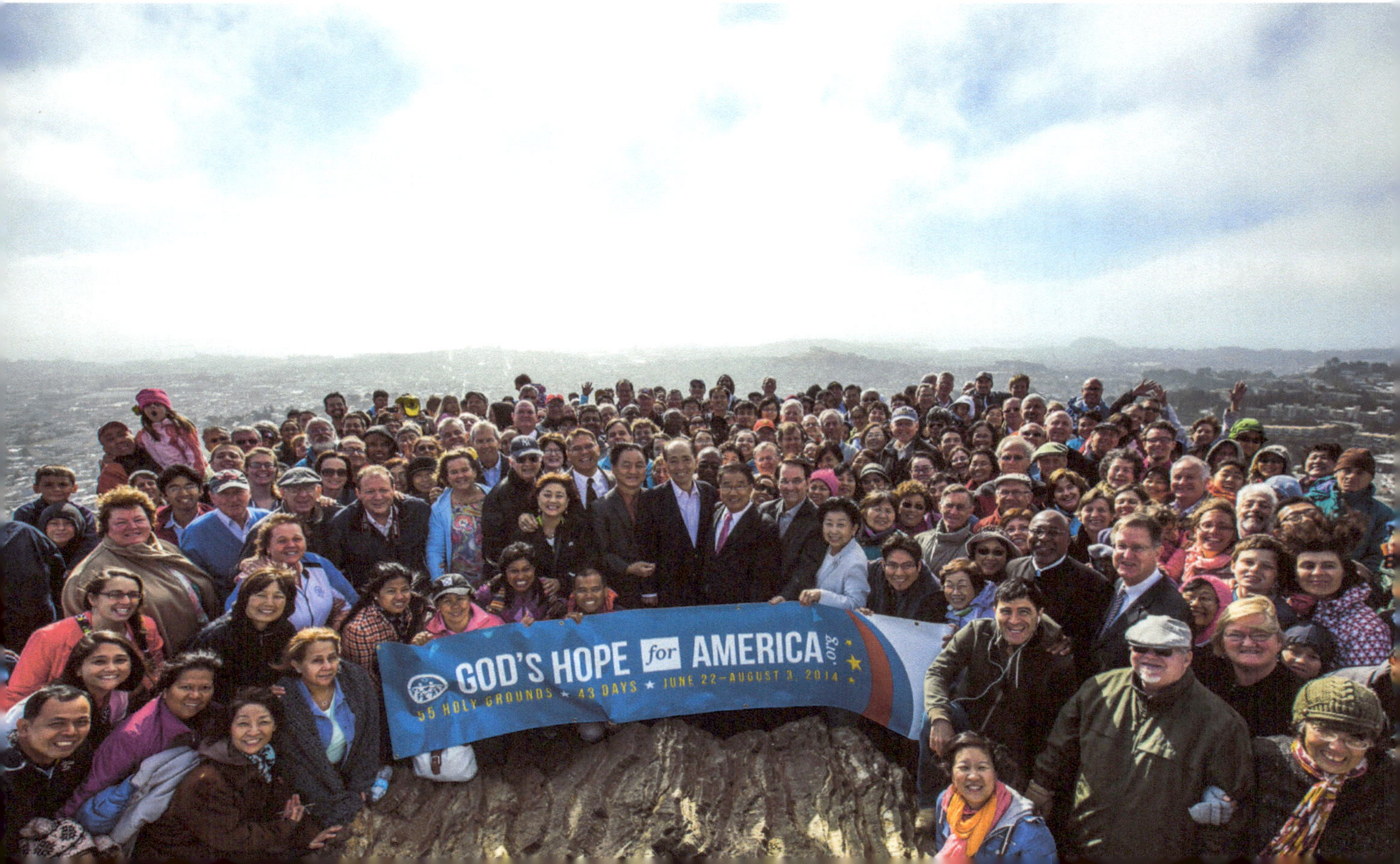
GOD'S HOPE for AMERICA .org
55 HOLY GROUNDS ★ 43 DAYS ★ JUNE 22–AUGUST 3, 2014

LOS ANGELES, CALIFORNIA

HOLY GROUND 2

EST: FEBRUARY 25, 1965
GPS COORDINATES: 34°07'12.8"N 118°18'18.0"W

GRIFFITH PARK
2800 E Observatory Rd.,
Los Angeles, CA 90027

LOCATION

The Los Angeles Holy Ground is located in Griffith Park, near the Hollywood sign. It lies on a plateau up a hill from the parking lot near picnic area No. 7.

JOURNAL ENTRY

Approximately 20 people piled into cars and drove in a procession to Griffith Park. At the foot of a big hill–a mountain almost–Rev. Moon walked around looking for the right spot to climb. Suddenly he shot up the side, and the stunned group scrambled desperately to catch up. Wasting no time, he chose a flat spot at the summit, among the tough shrubs and sandy soil, to perform the ceremony of blessing the Holy Ground.

To Mrs. Moon

I felt very close to the American members that I met in San Francisco and Los Angeles. I am well, with hardly any discomfort. Since they are all family members, I hardly feel any distance, so please know that I was at ease. From now on, America's fate depends upon their efforts.

-Rev. Moon, February 25, 1965, Las Vegas, NV

"TOGETHER, WE CAN MAKE
GOD'S PRESENCE IN AMERICA
A LIVING REALITY."
HOLY GROUND PILGRIMAGE
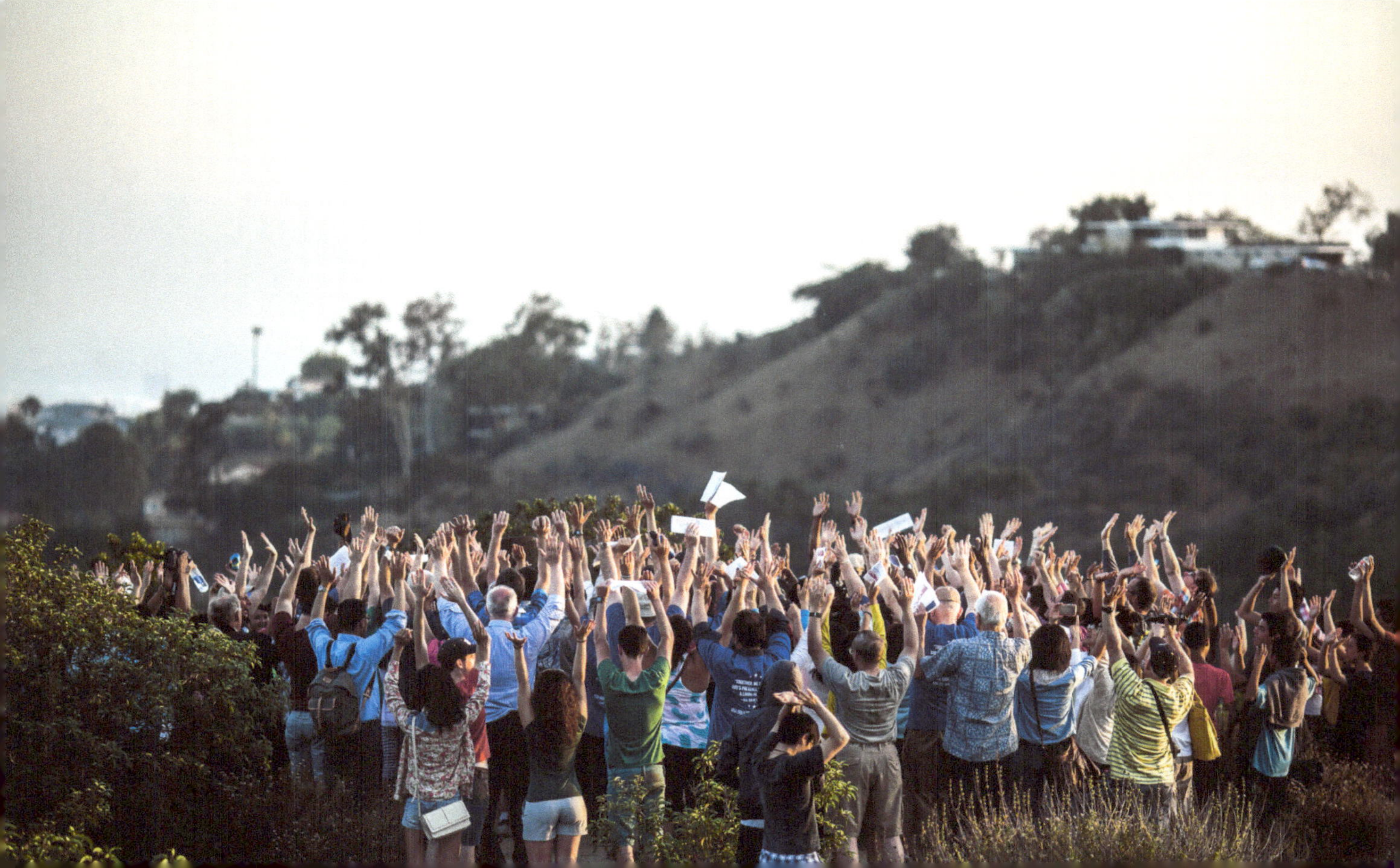

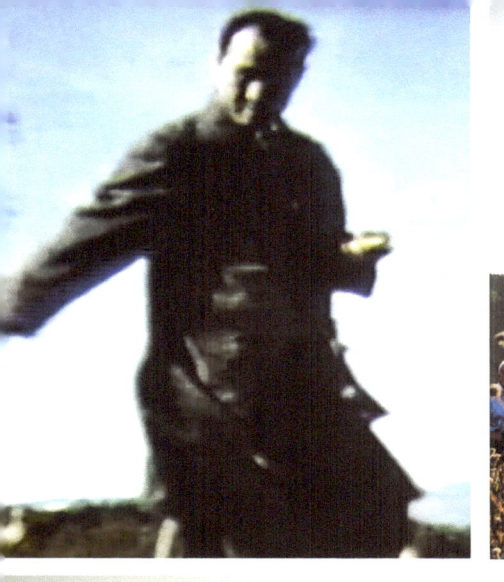

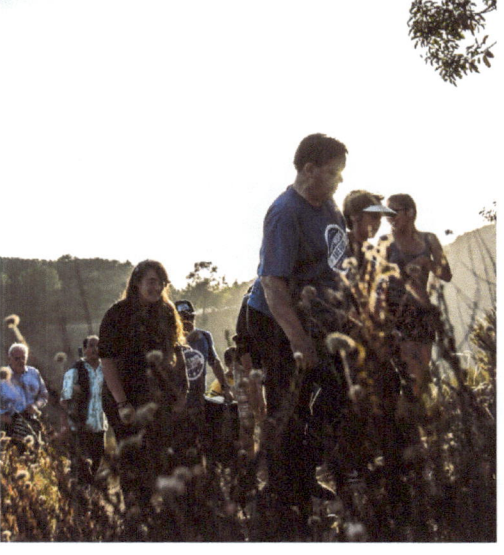

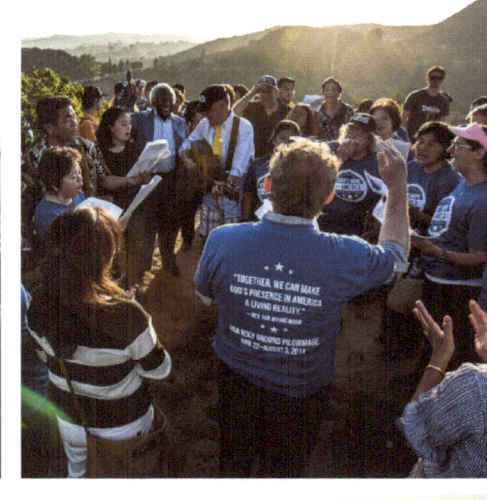

MT. WHITNEY, CALIFORNIA

HOLY GROUND  3

EST: FEBRUARY 25, 1965
GPS COORDINATES: 36°35'10.1"N 118°14'29.0"W

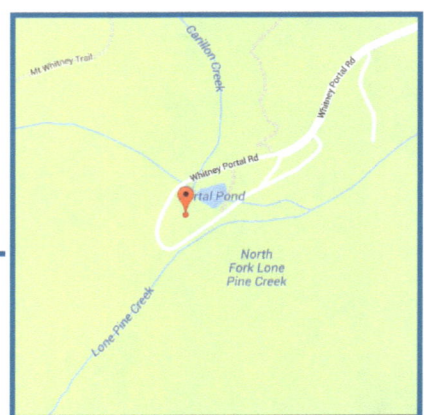

MT. WHITNEY
Whitney Portal Road,
Lone Pine, CA 93545

LOCATION

Mt. Whitney is the tallest mountain in the contiguous 48 states. The Holy Ground is located near the entrance to the peak at approximately 9,000 feet above sea level. It is marked by a grove of pine trees on this mountain.

JOURNAL ENTRY

Rev. Moon was amazed at the vastness of the desert and the height of the mountains which jutted so sharply up alongside the highway as the group drove toward the town of Lone Pine, California, gateway to Mount Whitney, (elevation 14,495 feet). They stopped in a small grove of pine trees where Rev. Moon blessed the ground, which was then covered with a foot of snow.

To Mrs. Moon

We must possess heaven in our hearts and convey the heart of heaven to others. Please comfort the people who are close to you and develop your motherly presence. I will also work to complete this tour with strength.

-Rev. Moon, February 15, 1965, San Francisco, CA

GOD'S HOPE
FOR AMERICA
GOD'S HOPE
AMERICA
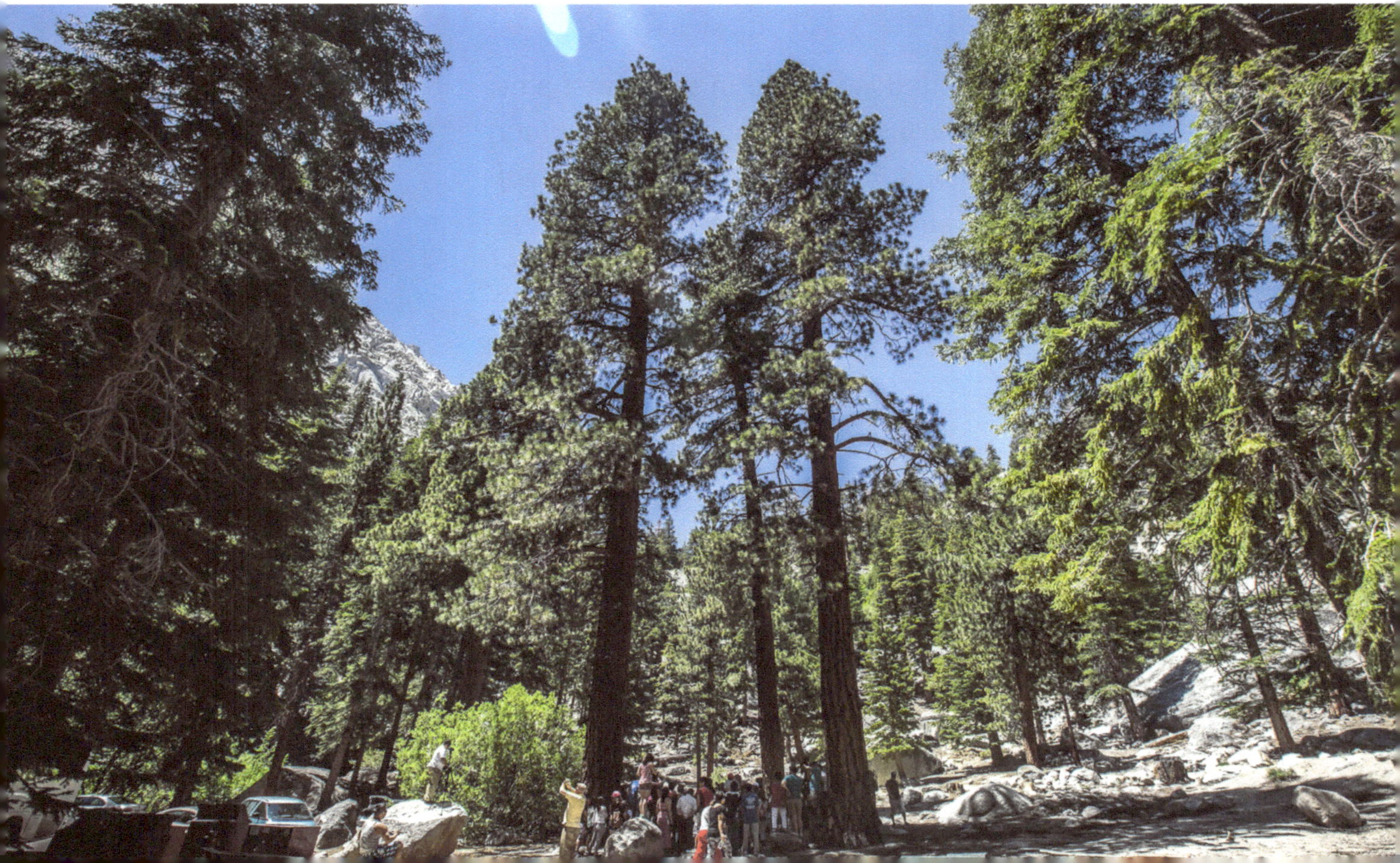

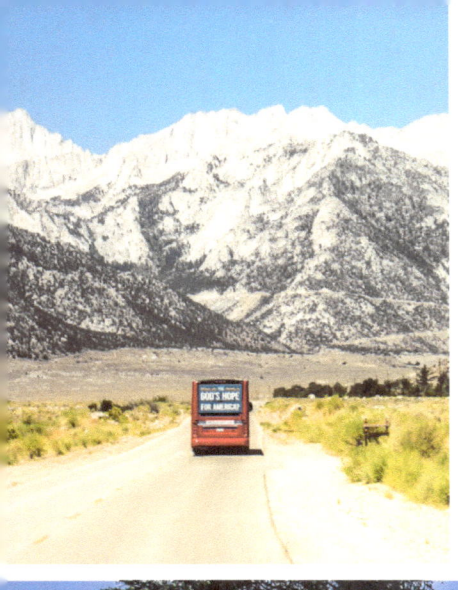

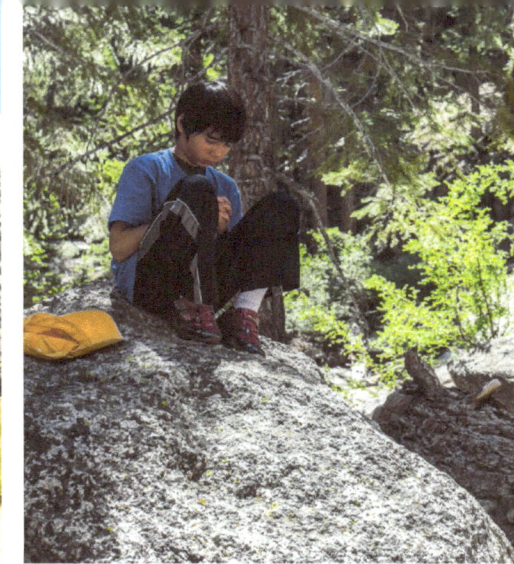

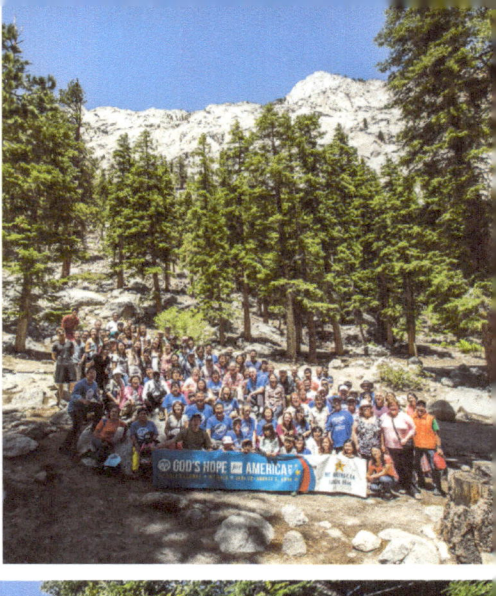

DEATH VALLEY, CALIFORNIA

HOLY GROUND

EST: FEBRUARY 25, 1965
GPS COORDINATES: 36°13'47.9"N 116°46'05.2"W

DEATH VALLEY
Badwater Basin, Death Valley National Park, CA

LOCATION

The Death Valley Holy Ground is located in the lowest area of a salt flat, 282 feet below sea level, approximately four miles from Badwater. Wear sunscreen and keep hydrated! The temperatures in Death Valley can reach well above 100 degrees in the summertime. Keep an empty water bottle on the drive down. Watch what below-water pressure does to it.

JOURNAL ENTRY

From the heavenly heights of Mount Whitney to the infernal depths of Death Valley, the group descended until they reached the lowest point of land in the Western Hemisphere: Badwater Basin in Death Valley. There, Rev. Moon blessed the ground, covering it with Holy Salt. On that day, the United States had four Holy Grounds, all in California.

To Mrs. Moon

I only pray with hope that this large American continent will be set ablaze with heaven's fire. … I deeply realized that the future destiny of the Unification Church is to fight here in America.

-Rev. Moon, February 25, 1965, Las Vegas, NV

LAS VEGAS, NEVADA

HOLY GROUND 5

EST: FEBRUARY 25, 1965

GPS COORDINATES: 36°10'56.8"N 115°07'57.6"W

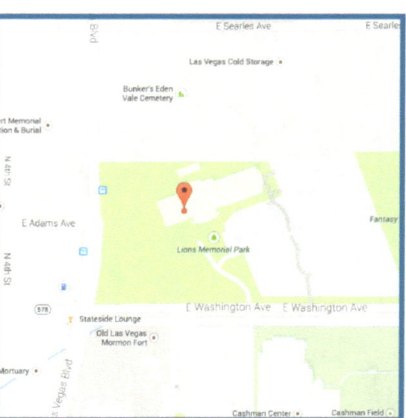

HOLY SITE
555 East Washington Ave., Las Vegas, NV 89101

LOCATION

The Las Vegas Holy Ground was originally located in Lions Memorial Park. It is now covered by the Grant Sawyer Office Building at 555 E. Washington Ave., but this is open to the public.

JOURNAL ENTRY

In Las Vegas, Rev. Moon stayed at the Stardust, a very lavish motor hotel on "The Strip." The neon lights of the gambling casinos downtown were so bright that they made a whole section of the city appear literally as bright as day! The next day (February 26), he blessed a Holy Ground and went quickly on toward the Phoenix Center in Arizona.

WHILE IN THE AREA

- Stop by the International Peace Education Center, envisioned by Rev. and Mrs. Moon as a facility where peace education is given to leaders from around the world.

MR MOON VISIT LAS VEGAS IN 1965 (CITY HALL)

PACIFIC

Rev. and Mrs. Moon loved Lake Mead Marina near Las Vegas. Though the temperatures here are swelteringly hot, they would take out their boat and fish for carp and enjoy the beauty of this little desert oasis. The 2014 God's Hope for America pilgrimage stopped here briefly to take in its beauty.

PHOENIX, ARIZONA

HOLY GROUND 6

EST: FEBRUARY 26, 1965
GPS COORDINATES: 33°25'13.9"N 111°56'0.2"W

ARIZONA STATE UNIVERSITY
425 E. University Dr., Tempe, AZ 85281

LOCATION

The Phoenix Holy Ground was originally located in Encanto Park, which now has many small canals located across the original site. A second Holy Ground was therefore dedicated on the Tempe Campus of Arizona State University. The new Holy Ground is marked by an Aleppo pine tree in a grassy area between the University Club, the Old Main, and Piper Writers' house.

JOURNAL ENTRY

When they arrived in Phoenix it was late at night. Rev. Moon chose to stay at the local church center. It was a small house. An area was cleared in the little living room and all seven travelers slept on the floor. The next morning, in a warm sunny park, Rev. Moon chose a sapling to be the center of the Holy Ground.

WHILE IN THE AREA

- The magnificent Grand Canyon is of course a must-see, as is Sedona.
- The John Wayne shoot-'em-up movie "The Train Robbers" was filmed on the route from the Grand Canyon to Phoenix in 1973. It is a movie well-liked by True Parents and was watched on the bus during the 2014 tour.

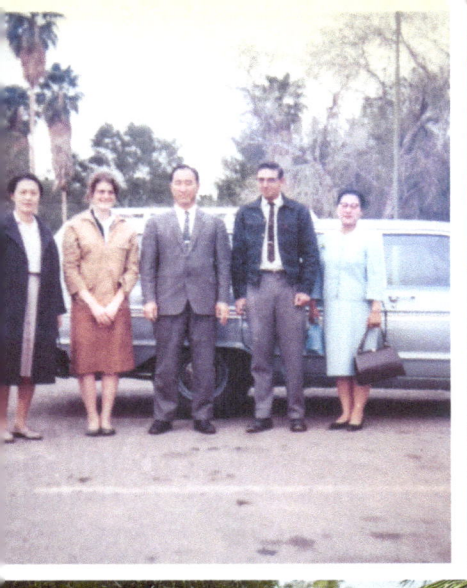

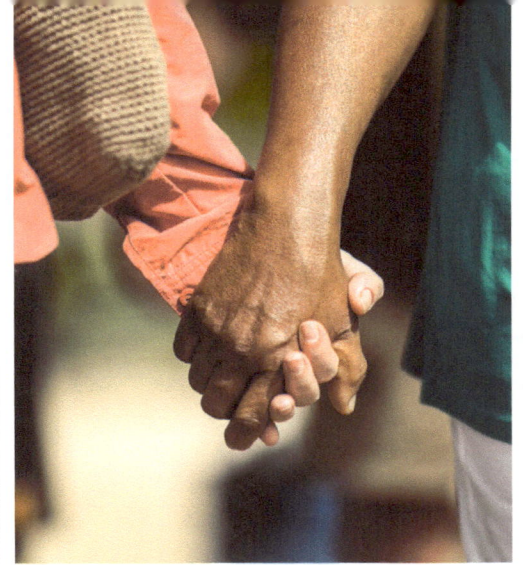

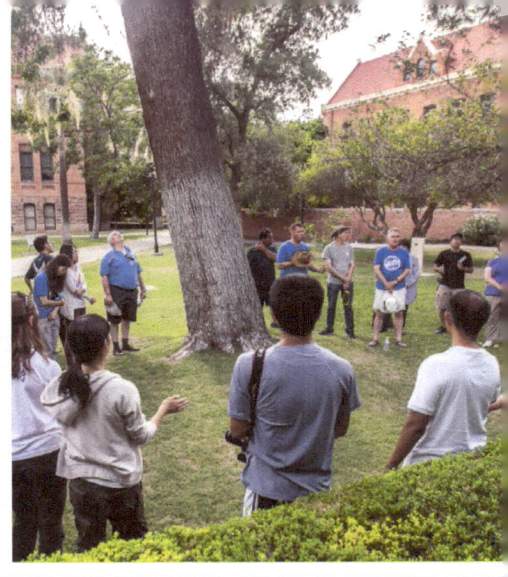

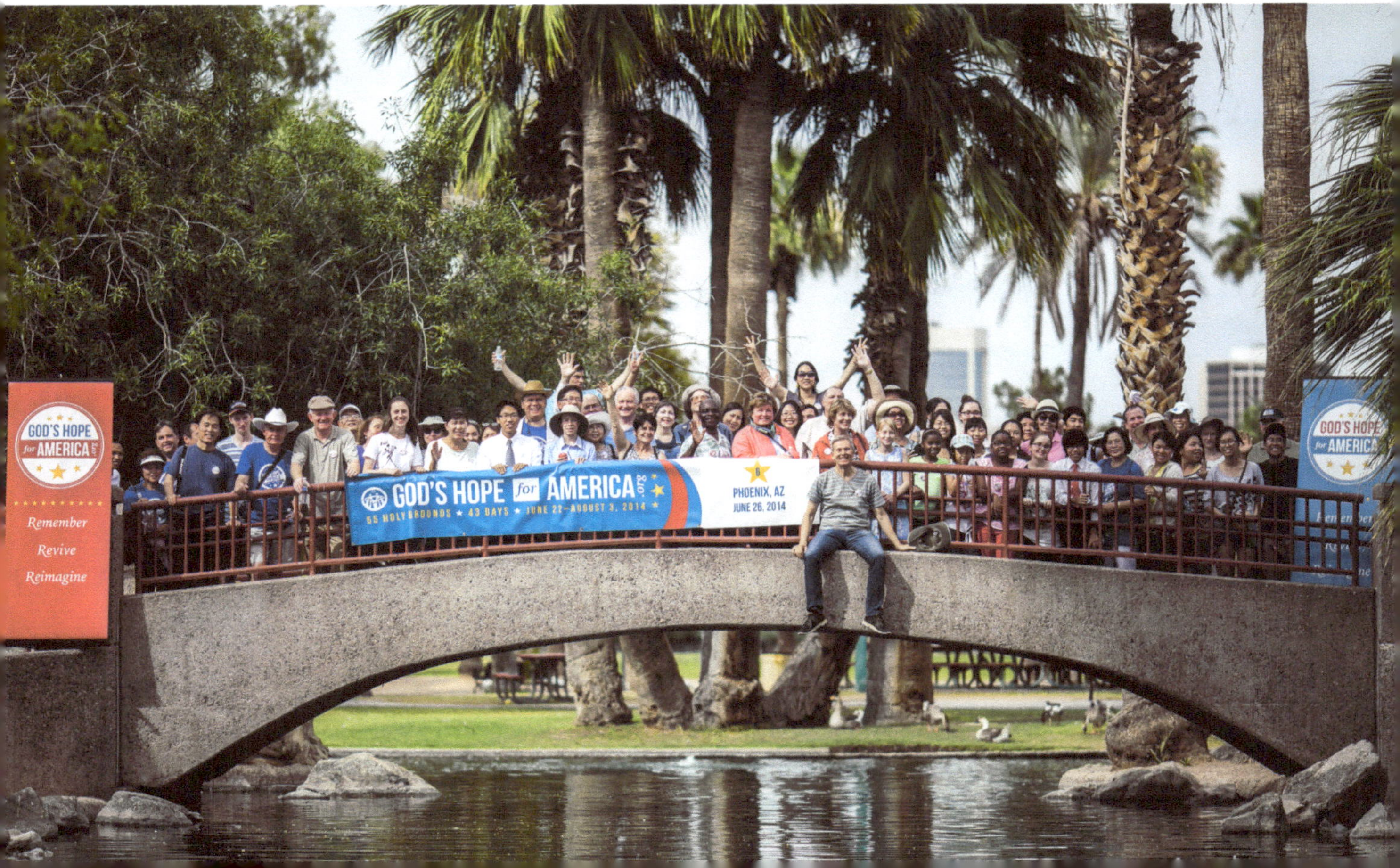
GOD'S HOPE for AMERICA
Remember
Revive
Reimagine
GOD'S HOPE for AMERICA
55 HOLY GROUNDS ★ 43 DAYS ★ JUNE 22–AUGUST 3, 2014
PHOENIX, AZ
JUNE 26, 2014
GOD'S HOPE for AMERICA

"It is the time to establish God's throne at the top of the Grand Canyon. People say how the Grand Canyon is great, but there has been no owner who can love it as God does. The Grand Canyon is an amazing creation."
—Rev. Moon, Grand Canyon, January 3, 2011

ALBUQUERQUE, NEW MEXICO

HOLY GROUND 7

EST: FEBRUARY 27, 1965

GPS COORDINATES: 35°04'35.1"N 106°37'57.6"W

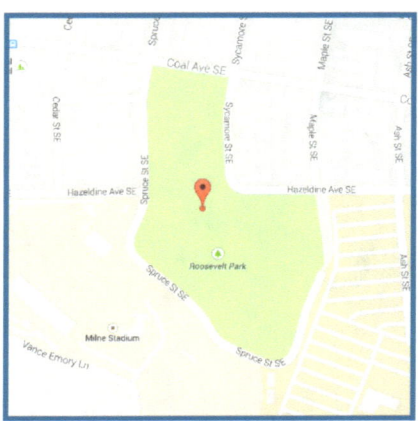

ROOSEVELT PARK
524 Sycamore St. SE,
Albuquerque, NM 87106

LOCATION

The Albuquerque Holy Ground is located in Roosevelt Park, adjacent to Central New Mexico Community College. The Holy Ground is marked by a tree near the top of a hill to the west of several college buildings.

JOURNAL ENTRY

Rev. Moon blessed a Holy Ground in Albuquerque after having some difficulty in finding a pebble and some dirt at City Hall, since it was surrounded by a concrete sidewalk. However, they chipped a piece of stone off the corner of City Hall, dug some dirt out from between the cracks of the sidewalk, and continued on their way.

To Mrs. Moon

As I anticipated, the American members who joined us for the Principle are the same as church members in Korea. When it comes to the Will, we are no different.

-Rev. Moon, February 25, 1965, Las Vegas, NV

GATEWAY
OF AMERICA

REGION B

TRAVEL TIME: FEBRUARY 28, 1965 - MARCH 10, 1965

The South is unique: its history is deeply rich but marred by pain and suffering. From Dallas, Texas, to Little Rock, Arkansas, and from Mobile, Alabama, to Atlanta, Georgia, the Gateway of America section of the pilgrimage is an example of the beauty of God's creation that is etched with the struggles of the history of restoration.

"To be an American does not depend on what race you are, what belief you have, or what cultural background you are from. It is only in this nation that no matter where you are from, you can say, 'This is my country.' God protected this land, for that very purpose."

—Rev. Moon, "God's Hope for America," Washington, D.C. October 21, 1973

B GATEWAY

CHECKLIST OF HOLY GROUNDS

- [ ] Dallas, TX
- [ ] Oklahoma City, OK
- [ ] Kansas City, KS
- [ ] St. Louis, MO
- [ ] Paducah, KY
- [ ] Memphis, TN
- [ ] Little Rock, AR
- [ ] New Orleans, LA
- [ ] Mobile, AL
- [ ] Tampa, FL
- [ ] Miami, FL
- [ ] Savannah, GA

DALLAS, TEXAS

HOLY GROUND

EST: FEBRUARY 28, 1965
GPS COORDINATES: 32°50'13.7"N 96°42'51.1"W

WHITE ROCK LAKE PARK
690 E. Lawther Dr.,
Dallas, TX 75218

LOCATION

The Dallas Holy Ground is in White Rock Lake Park. It is located about 75 yards from the shore of the lake. The Holy Ground is marked by a small leaf elm tree that stands north of a small parking lot and picnic area.

JOURNAL ENTRY

On the way to Dallas, Texas, the group experienced just how dry and brutal Texas really was. A storm brewed, but not a rainstorm; it was a raging dust storm. The earth of Texas suddenly whirled up, building into thicker and higher clouds. It sifted into the car until everything was covered with grit. They could hardly see where they were going, but they kept moving anyway. It seemed like an eternity before the storm gave up. Neither snow nor rain nor sleet nor hail—nor dust—would stop the progress of this heavenly mission. Rev. Moon then blessed a Holy Ground in Dallas.

To Mrs. Moon

It is definitely true that nothing can stop me from thinking about (our children) no matter how far away I am from them. Please be careful in the middle of your pregnancy and take care of your health. I am following my course, and my sense of duty is directing me to fulfill my responsibility in America.

-Rev. Moon, February 25, 1965, Las Vegas, NV

OKLAHOMA CITY, OKLAHOMA

HOLY GROUND 9

EST: MARCH 1, 1965
GPS COORDINATES: 35°29'20.5"N 97°30'12.6"W

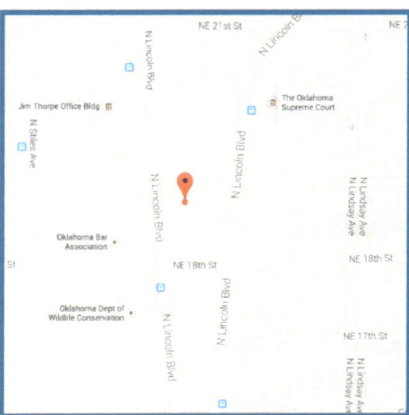

LINCOLN PARK
1892 N Lincoln Blvd.,
Oklahoma City, OK 73105

LOCATION

The Oklahoma City Holy Ground is in Lincoln Park. It is located in a field near a picnic area and parking lot. The original tree marking the location is gone.

JOURNAL ENTRY

The group drove from Dallas to Oklahoma City, encountering in Oklahoma the scenery of rolling hills and flat land, dusted lightly with new-fallen snow. After a two-day visit, during which Rev. Moon saw his first buffalo near the city of Anadarko, they traveled through a flat prairie north and east along the 80 mph freeway to Kansas City, Kansas. Rev. Moon blessed a Holy Ground in City Park amid picnickers and canoers.

To Mrs. Moon

Whenever I think of you doing your very best to fulfill your responsibility as a young woman with a delicate frame, I believe that heaven will look upon you tenderly. Now my thoughts move across the Pacific Ocean to Korea, where I miss the people and the land that I love.

-Rev. Moon, March 6, 1965, Little Rock, AR

GOD'S HOPE
AMERICA

"TOGETHER, WE CAN MAKE
GOD'S PRESENCE IN AMERICA
A LIVING REALITY."
— REV. SUN MYUNG MOON
USA HOLY GROUND PILGRIMAGE
JUNE 22—AUGUST 3, 2014

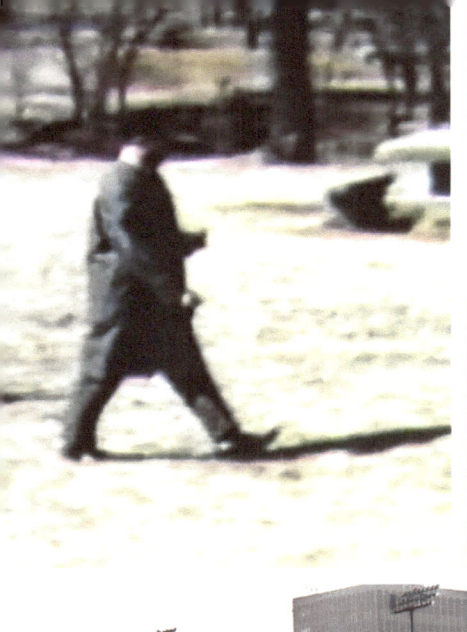

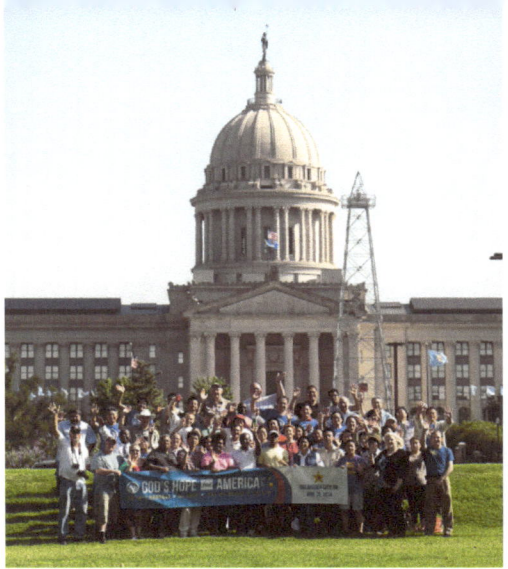

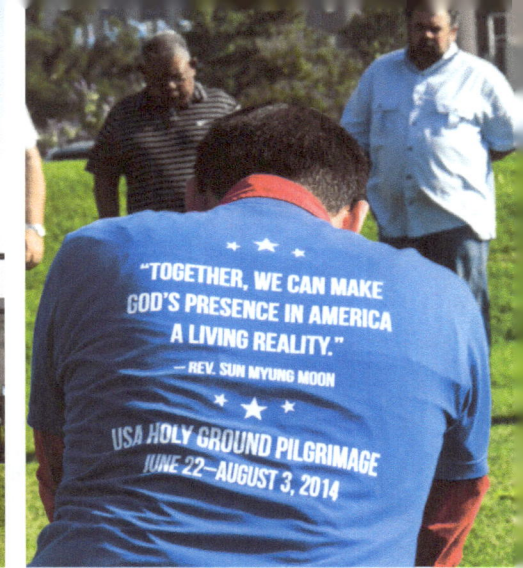

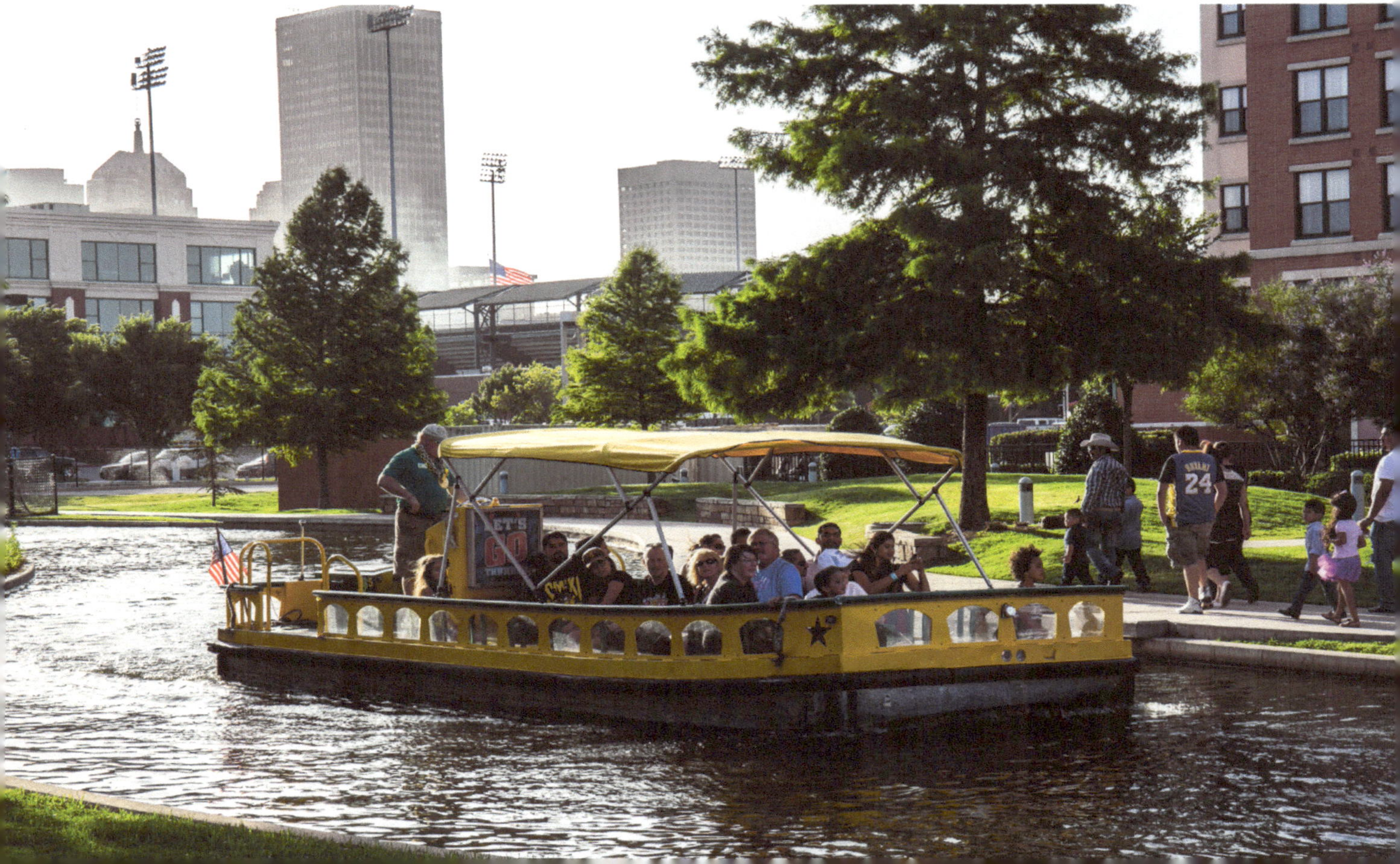

KANSAS CITY, KANSAS

HOLY GROUND 10

EST: MARCH 3, 1965
GPS COORDINATES: 39°06'01.1"N 94°39'57.5"W

CITY PARK
2601 Park Dr.,
Kansas City, KS 66102

LOCATION

The Kansas City Holy Ground is located in City Park. It is on top of a hill overlooking an industrial park and train yards. The Holy Ground is marked by two trees with branches that have grown into each other. Stop by Tall Grass Prairie National Preserve in Strong City, Kansas while you're here. The tall grass is the very last remnant (less than 3%) of the vast prairies that once covered the Midwest.

JOURNAL ENTRY

The 80 mile-per-hour Interstate 80 was a welcome relief after the potholes and narrow roads of Oklahoma, and they sped through the flat winter fields of Kansas where corn and wheat would soon thrive. In City Park of Kansas City, Rev. Moon blessed the Holy Ground.

To Mrs. Moon

It is natural for people who are separated by distance to yearn for the ones we love. ... I came here saying that I would not write letters, but I felt sorry when it occurred to me that you might be expecting them, so I am quickly writing to you. Our mission is becoming greater and greater.

-Rev. Moon, March 6, 1965, Little Rock, AR

ST. LOUIS, MISSOURI

HOLY GROUND

EST: MARCH 4, 1965

GPS COORDINATES: 38°38'29.7"N 90°17'44.1"W

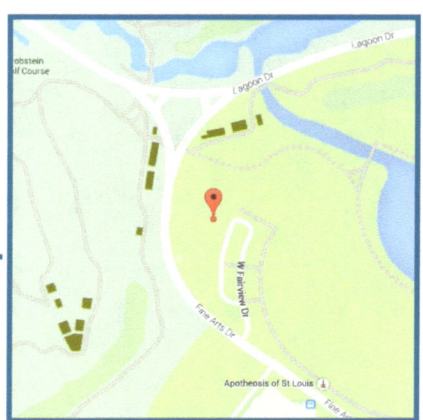

FOREST PARK
300 W. Fairview Dr.,
St. Louis, MO 63110

LOCATION

The St. Louis Holy Ground is located at the Norman K. Probstein Golf Course. It is near a large circular concrete pad, just north of the art museum, overlooking a man-made pond. This is the city of the famous Gateway Arch! Visit this landmark on Washington Street downtown, or see it from across the river at Malcolm Martin Memorial Park.

JOURNAL ENTRY

There were just two Unificationist couples living in St. Louis, so what an occasion this was for them. As everyone stood among some cedar trees in Forest Park, the cold wind cut through their coats, and their fingers and toes soon felt frozen. Rev. Moon paced off the Holy Ground a little faster than before. The four Missouri members were amazed to notice how completely Rev. Moon focused on what he was doing.

To Mrs. Moon

During this tour, I find myself thinking of the tours I did in Korea before 1960.

O, America when will you bend your big body and bow in service to heaven?

-Rev. Moon, March 6, 1965, Little Rock, AR

GOD'S HOPE
AMERICA
GOD'S PRESE
A LIVING
USA HOLY GROUND
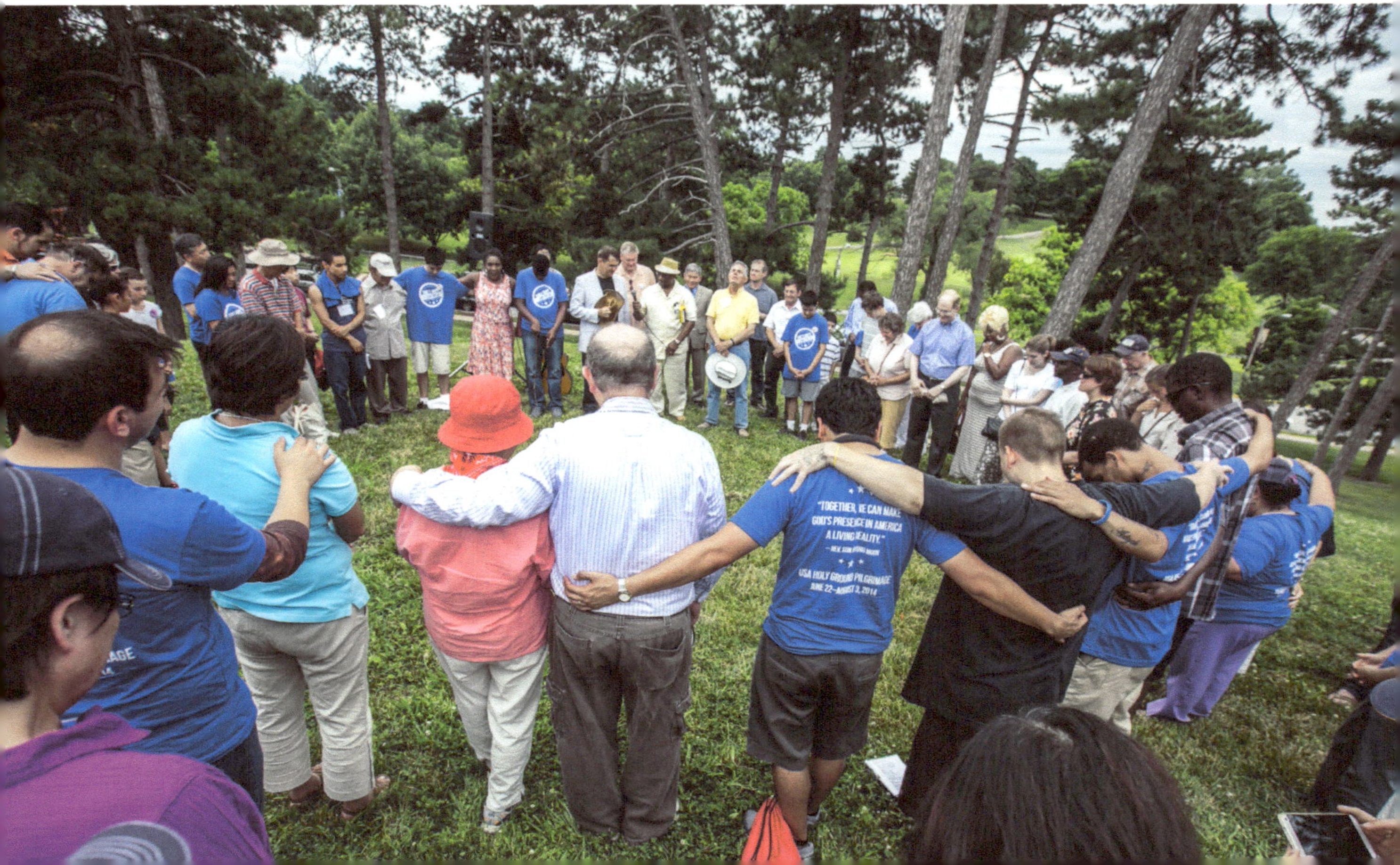
CAN MAKE
GOD'S PRESENCE IN AMERICA
A LIVING REALITY."
USA HOLY GROUND PILGRIMAGE
JUNE 22—AUGUST 3, 2014

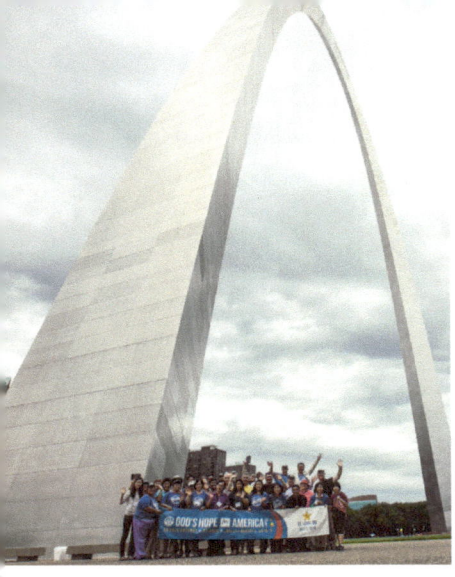

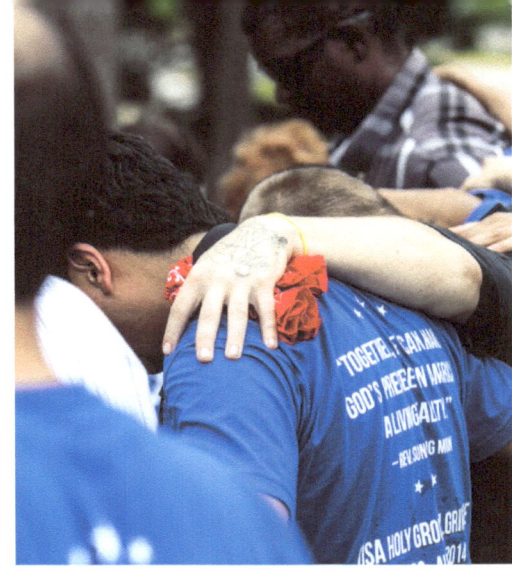

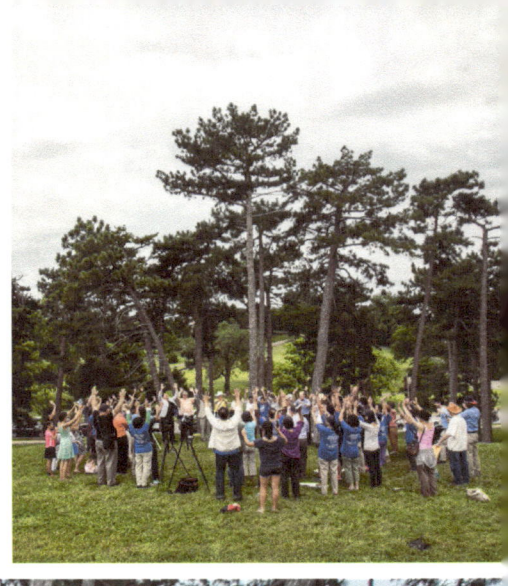

PADUCAH, KENTUCKY

HOLY GROUND

EST: MARCH 4, 1965
GPS COORDINATES: 37°05'06.1"N 88°38'18.3"W

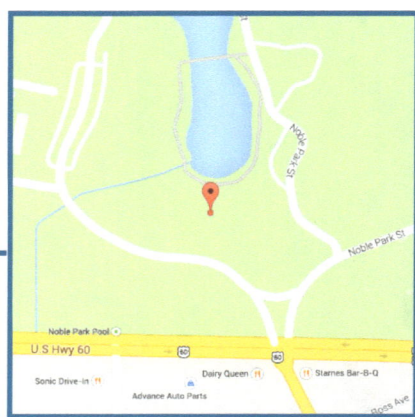

NOBLE PARK
2915 Park Ave.,
Paducah, KY 42001

LOCATION

The Paducah Holy Ground is located in Noble Park. It is marked by the largest and oldest tree in the park. It is also 10 minutes away from Metropolis, Illinois, home to the comic book hero Superman. Say "Hi" to the Man of Steel as you pass by!

JOURNAL ENTRY

Heading back south, the little band of travelers looked forward to leaving the snow and ice behind. There wasn't time to drive to Kentucky's capital, Frankfort, so they just drove into the western tip of Kentucky where snow still covered the ground and blessed a Holy Ground in Paducah.

To Mrs. Moon

I cannot help but worry about your heavy responsibilities. Please study hard, keep your body healthy and pray a lot. I feel sorry that you have such a burden despite being so young and delicate and I am grateful to you for following me so well. I entreat you to stand large and victorious before heaven.

-Rev. Moon, March 6, 1965, Little Rock, AR

MEMPHIS, TENNESSEE

HOLY GROUND ⭐ 13

EST: MARCH 5, 1965
GPS COORDINATES: 35°08'39.2"N 89°59'36.3"W

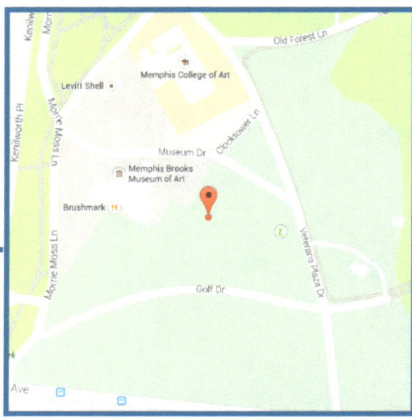

BROOKS MUSEUM
1934 Poplar Ave.,
Memphis, TN 38104

LOCATION

The Memphis Holy Ground is located at the Brooks Museum. There, a cedar tree situated between two double-trunk magnolia trees marks the Holy Ground.

JOURNAL ENTRY

From Paducah, they went south to Memphis, Tennessee, arriving at night. Looking for a suitable piece of land in a pitch-black wooded park was quite normal for them by then, but the local police doubted the normality of their intentions, and interrogated them about their plans. The policeman accepted the explanation and left, slightly bewildered. Rev. Moon performed the ceremony without delay, and within minutes they were speeding into the countryside once again.

WHILE IN THE AREA

- Memphis is where Dr. Martin Luther King Jr. gave his final speech, "I've been to the mountaintop." Visit the Civil Rights Museum in Memphis and make Dr. King's world-changing story a part of your prayers when considering what is God's Hope for America.

MARTIN LUTHER KING JR
LET US SLAY HIM
GENESIS 37:19-20
DAVID ABERNATHY PRESIDENT
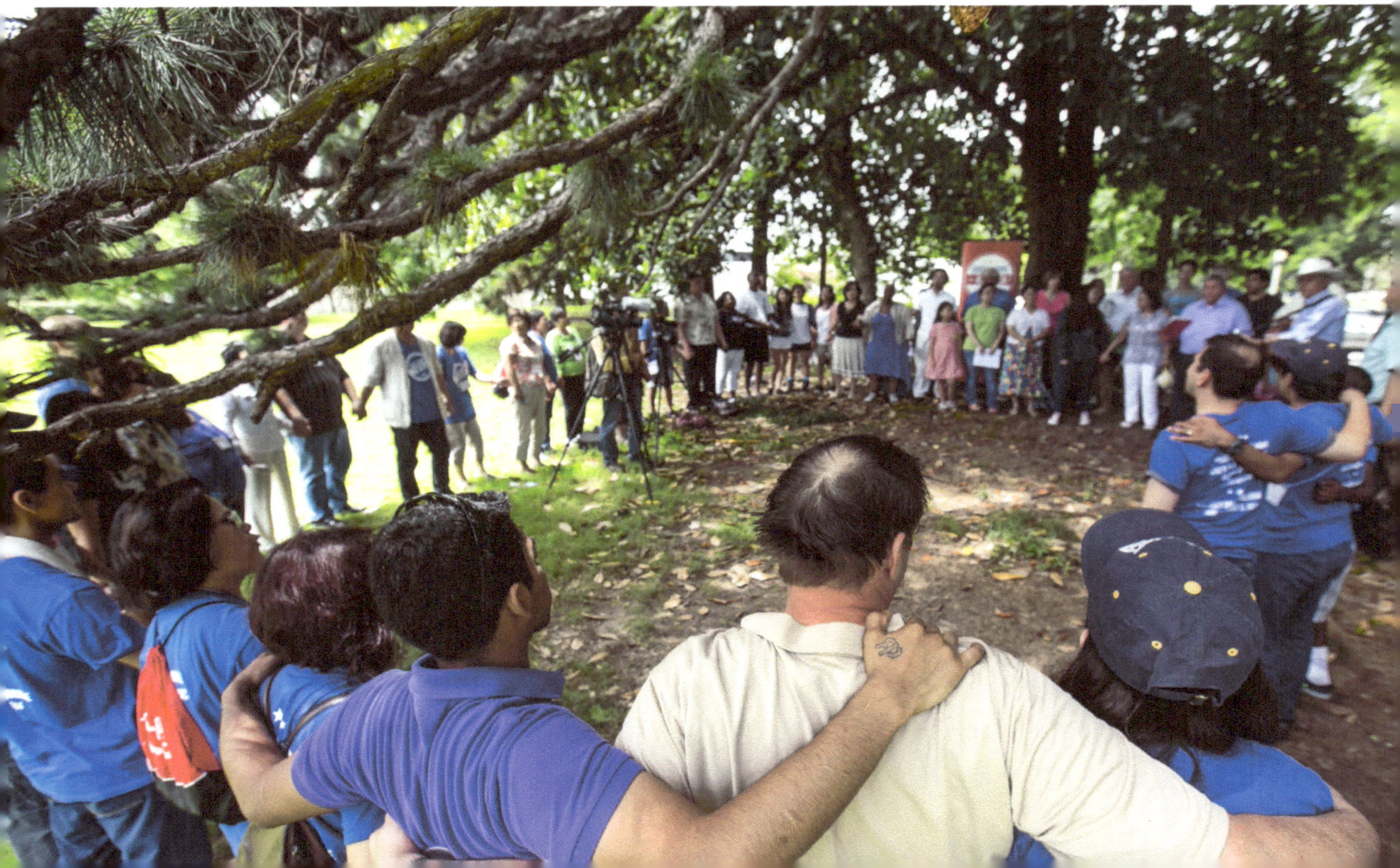

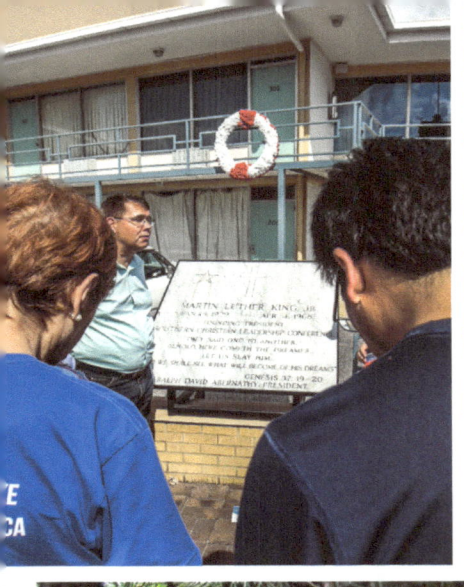

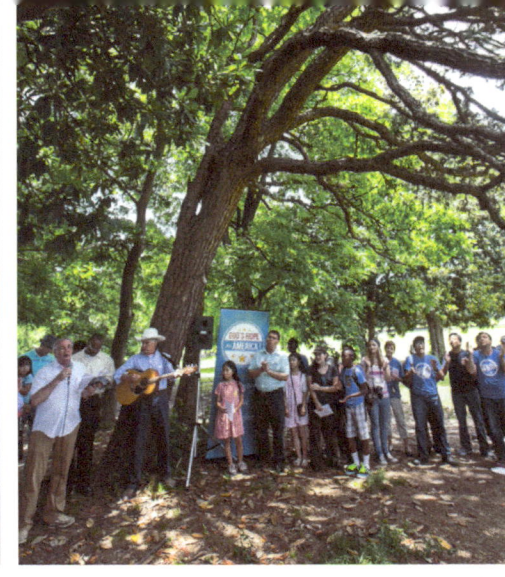

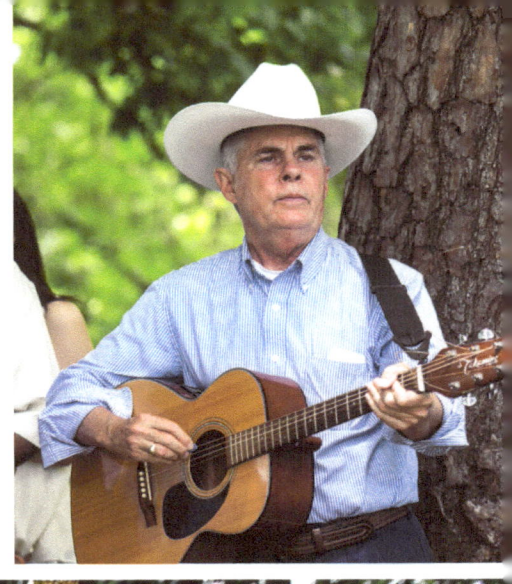

LITTLE ROCK, ARKANSAS

HOLY GROUND 14

EST: MARCH 6, 1965
GPS COORDINATES: 34°44'54.0"N 92°19'42.3"W

LOCATION

The Little Rock Holy Ground is located in War Memorial Park. It is marked by an oak tree on a hill west of gate No. 4 of the War Memorial Stadium. Take this opportunity to see the MacArthur Park and MacArthur Museum, named in honor of General Douglas MacArthur, who was born in Little Rock. Rev. Moon also stopped here to visit during his original tour, as the Korean War Memorial is also located here.

JOURNAL ENTRY

From Memphis they drove on to Little Rock, Arkansas, where they stayed overnight and blessed a Holy Ground at War Memorial Park in the morning. Several early morning golfers witnessed the ceremony, but appeared less disturbed than some of the travelers, who were worrying about the flight path of possible stray golf balls. Rev. Moon spread the Holy Salt and prayed, and then they were on their way.

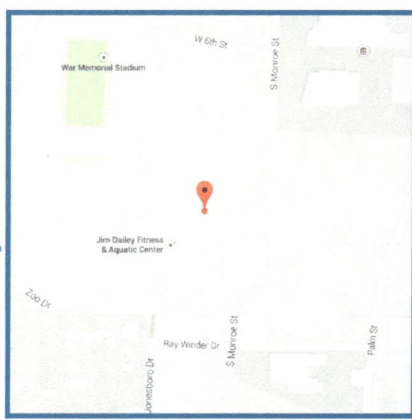

WAR MEMORIAL PARK
798 S. Monroe St.,
Little Rock, AR 72205

To Mrs. Moon

It is already March 6, 1:05 a.m., and I am writing to you after having traveled hundreds of miles, arriving at the Rose Motel in Little Rock, the state capital of Arkansas. This is the tenth state in which I have made a holy ground since coming to America.

-Rev. Moon, March 6, 1965, Little Rock, AR

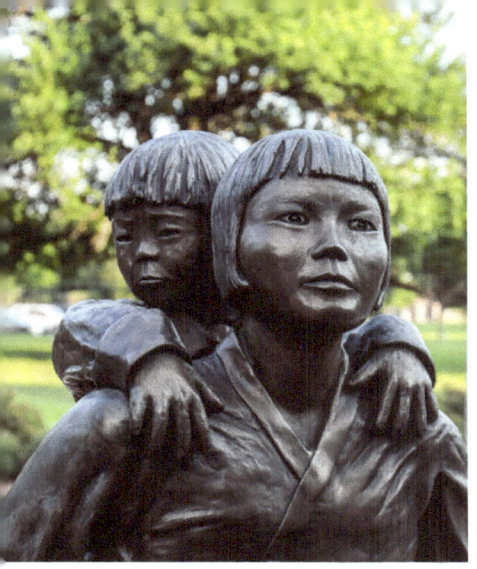

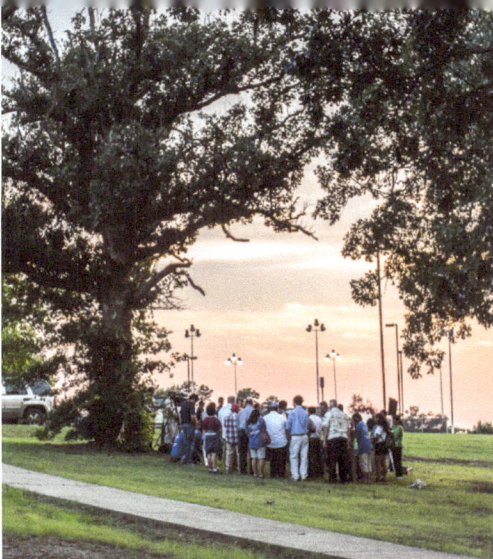

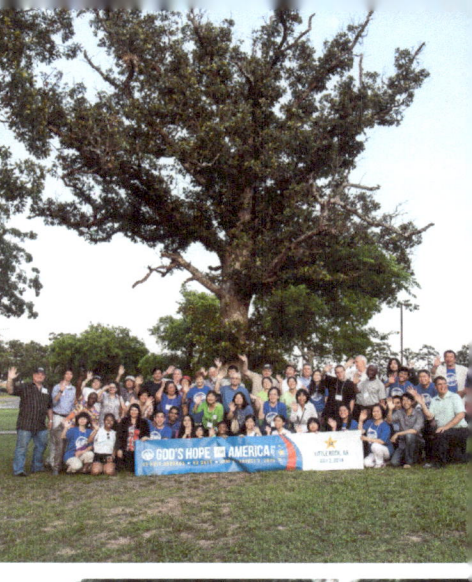

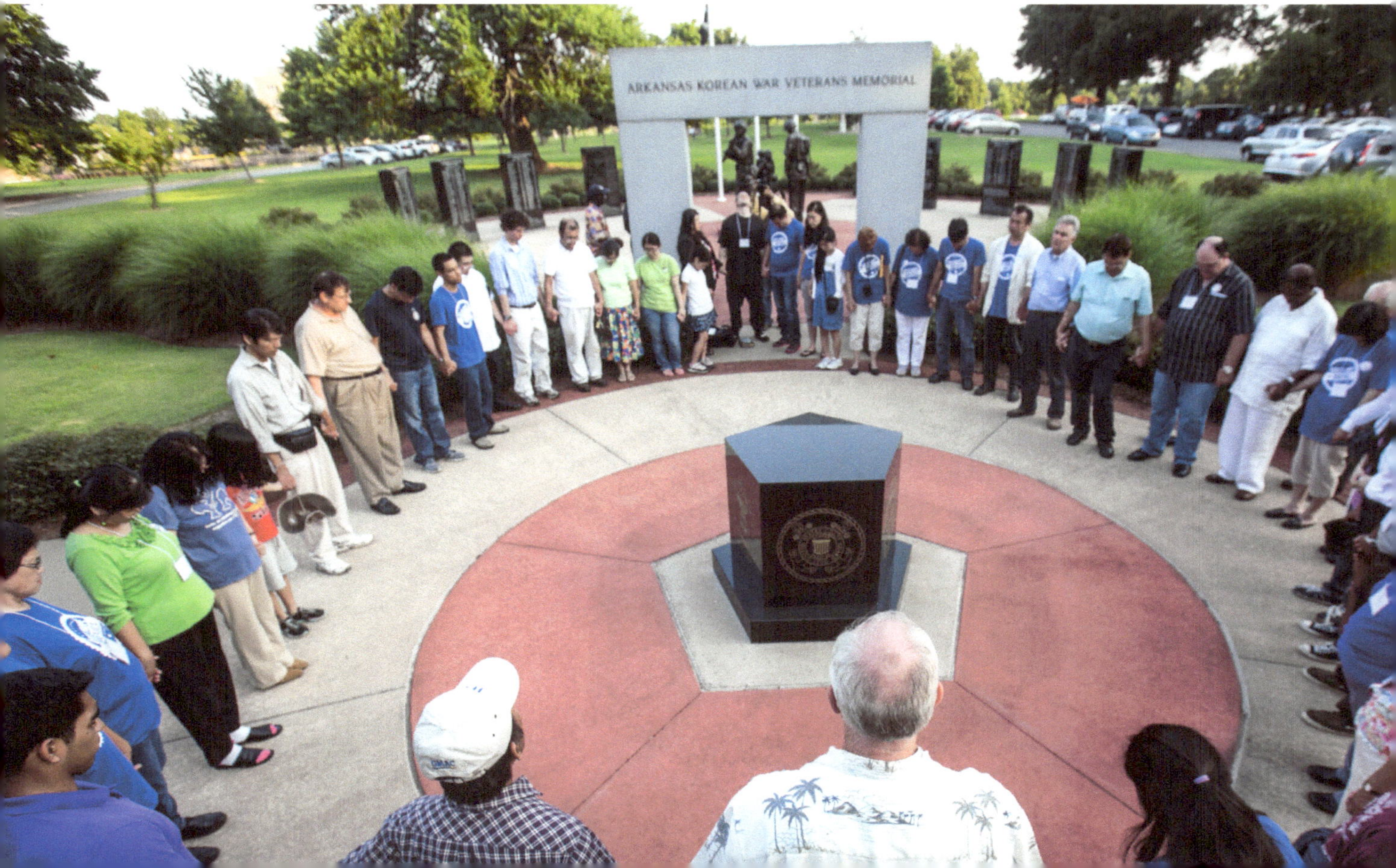
ARKANSAS KOREAN WAR VETERANS MEMORIAL

JACKSON, MISSISSIPPI

HOLY GROUND 15

EST: MARCH 6, 1965
GPS COORDINATES: 32°19'16.3"N 90°13'20.6"W

JACKSON ZOOLOGICAL PARK
2918 West Capitol St.,
Jackson, MS 39209

LOCATION

The Jackson Holy Ground is located in the Jackson Zoological Park in Livingston Park. It is across the lake from the park entrance near the zoo train track. The Holy Ground is marked by a tall pine tree with a piece of wood nailed to it approximately fifteen feet from the ground.

JOURNAL ENTRY

Hurrying quickly from state to state, they stopped at Livingston Park in Jackson, Mississippi, prayed and established the Holy Ground, then were on their way.

DID YOU KNOW?

- The God's Hope for America pilgrimage crossed the Mississippi River four times. Depending on where you begin your journey, you will cross the Mississippi River before or after you pass the Holy Ground in Jackson. Look out for this epic landmark!

NEW ORLEANS, LOUISIANA

HOLY GROUND 16

EST: MARCH 6, 1965
GPS COORDINATES: 29°59'3" N 90°5'45" W

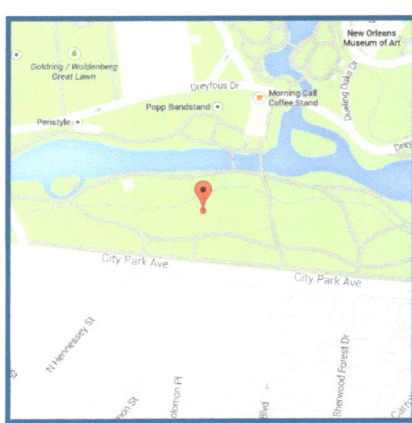

CITY PARK
1001-1025 City Park Ave.,
New Orleans, LA 70119

LOCATION

The New Orleans Holy Ground is in City Park. It is located near the Solomon Place entrance and is marked by a giant oak tree with a black concrete-filled hollow.

JOURNAL ENTRY

To reach New Orleans, they crossed the longest causeway in the United States, 29 miles across Lake Pontchartrain. For a while, they thought themselves to be steaming on the high seas. Only the tiny winking lights of bobbing ships greeted their eyes as they sped swiftly through the silent darkness of the great lake. The swamplands of Louisiana revealed still another side of America— green and stagnant and rather eerie, and yet there was a certain beauty about it. With the New Orleans Family, they blessed a Holy Ground in New Orleans on the night of their arrival.

WHILE IN THE AREA

- City Park is the sixth largest and seventh most-visited urban public park in the United States. Take time to find peace and reflect by the scenic bridges over the bayou and by sculptures and gardens. If you're going with your kids, don't miss out on the amusement park, the Storyland playground and the museum.

GOD'S HOPE for AMERICA!
Remember
Revive
Reimagine

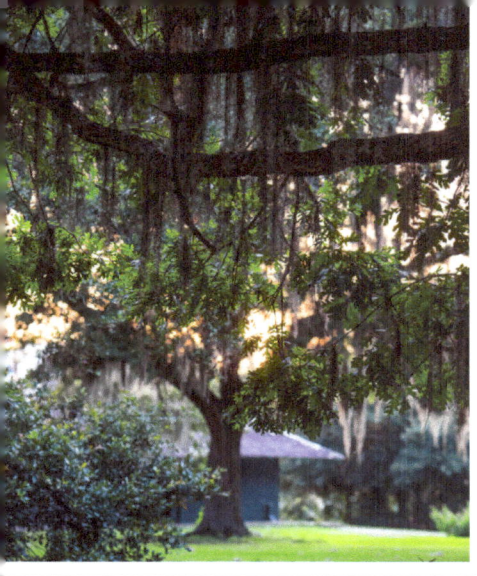

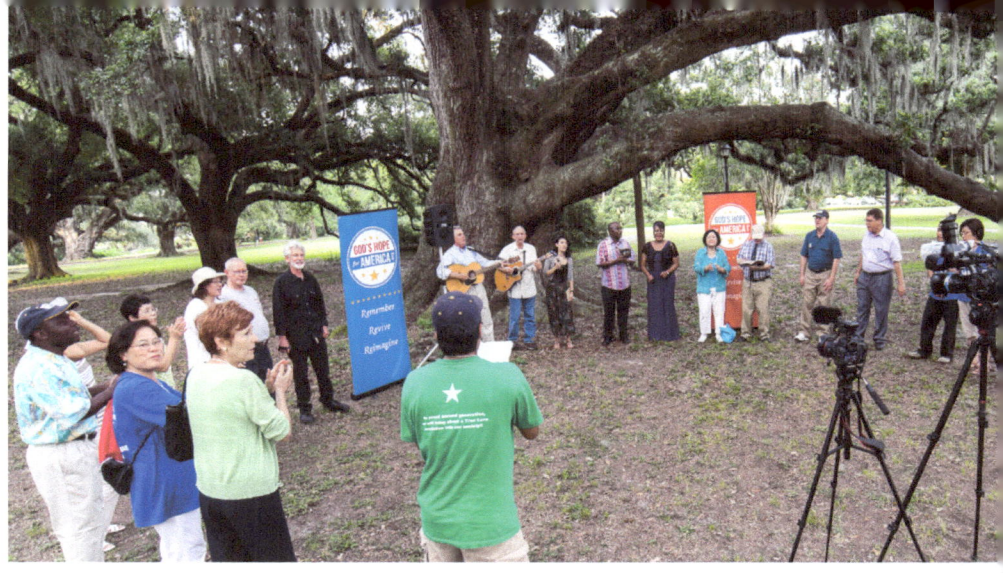

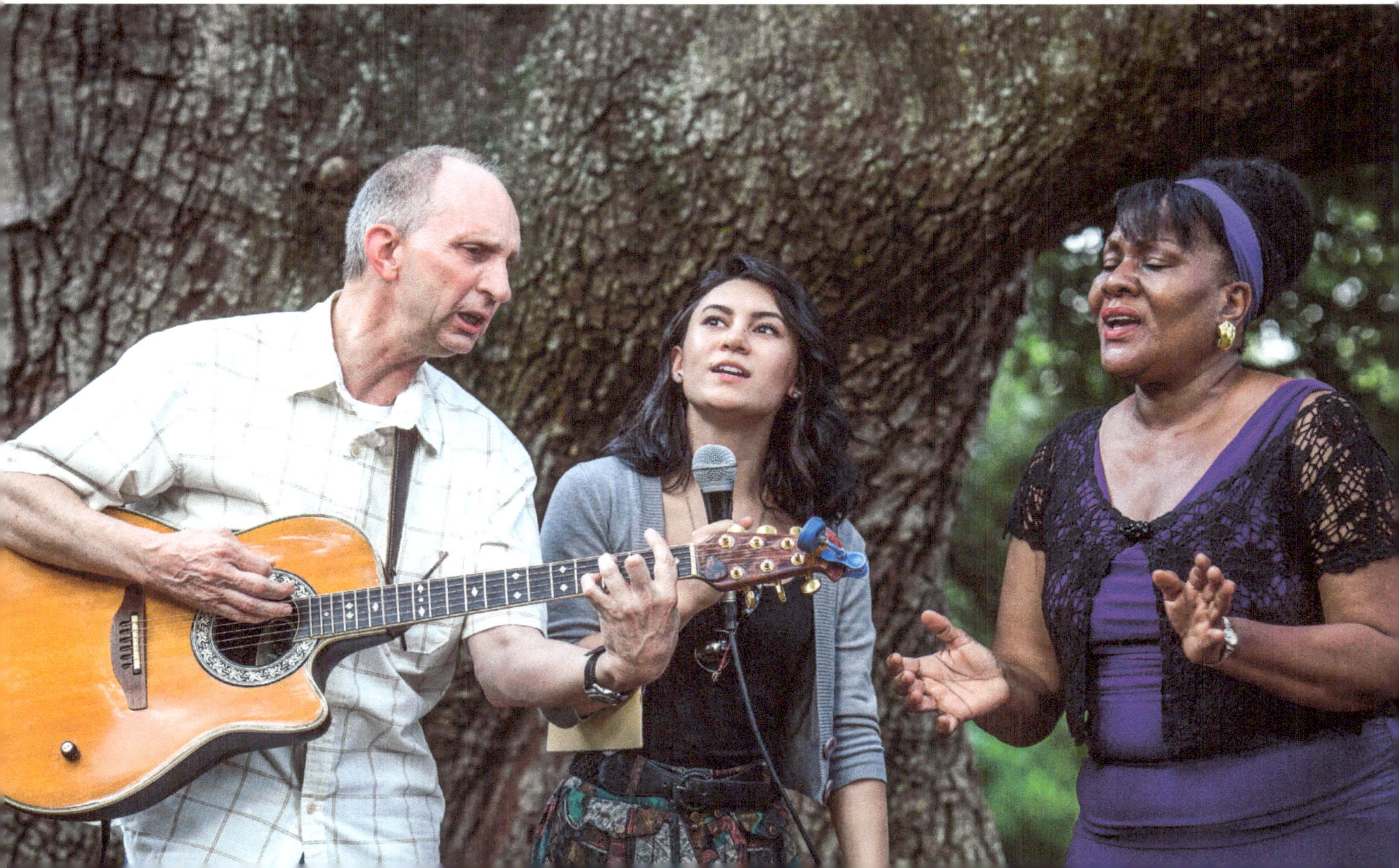

MOBILE, ALABAMA

HOLY GROUND ⭐ 17

EST: MARCH 7, 1965
GPS COORDINATES: 30°42'29" N 88°9'4" W

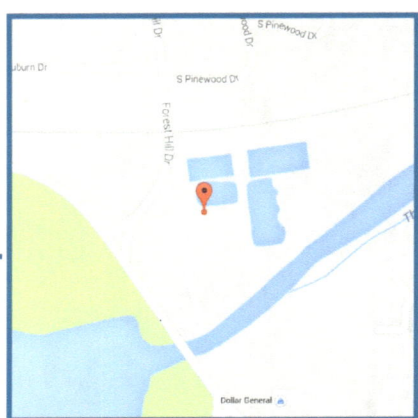

CHARLES WOOD JAPANESE GARDEN
900 Forest Hill Dr.,
Mobile, AL 36618

LOCATION

The Mobile Holy Ground is located near the corner of Forest Hill Dr. and Springhill Ave., across from Mobile Municipal Park. The Holy Ground is marked by a tall tree with a small plaque that reads, "Japanese Holy Ground 1965."

JOURNAL ENTRY

The sky was blue, and the Gulf of Mexico waters dancing in the sunny warmth of the day reflected the group's mood as they drove along the Louisiana-Alabama coast to Mobile, Alabama. There, Rev. Moon blessed a Holy Ground, and they hurried on to Tampa, Florida, through the swamplands of stunted trees, black water, thick undergrowth and Spanish moss. Rev. Moon made note of how green everything was, even in late winter, and wondered why there should be so much poverty.

WHILE IN THE AREA

- The Alabama Holy Ground is located in a former fish hatchery transformed into a lush Japanese garden over the last two decades.

- In Bayou La Batre, AL, visit Master Marine, completely rebuilt after Hurricane Katrina, and the International Oceanic Enterprise (IOE), where the air smells like shrimp and salt.

TAMPA, FLORIDA

HOLY GROUND 18

EST: MARCH 8, 1965
GPS COORDINATES: 28°00'44.1"N 82°28'10.3"W

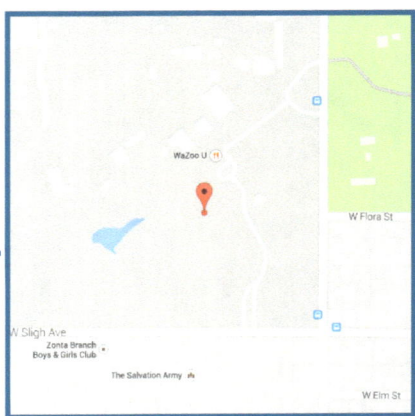

LOWRY PARK ZOO
1101 W Sligh Ave.,
Tampa, FL 33604

LOCATION

The Tampa Holy Ground is located just outside the zoo, in Lowry Park, at the edge of the main parking lot. It is in a grassy area south of the zoo and marked by a group of trees to the west of an open theater. The original pine trees are now gone.

JOURNAL ENTRY

The dancing blue waters of the Gulf of Mexico on their right made their spirits bright so early on the eleventh day after leaving Los Angeles. In Tampa's Lowry Park, among tall pines covered with Spanish moss, the Holy Ground was blessed.

HELPFUL TIPS

- If you have a large group with you, plan to hold a service at the amphitheater located near the Holy Ground. The zoo management will assist you.

- You can't leave Tampa, Florida, without taking a dip in the warm Gulf waters. There is no other body of water like it in the United States!

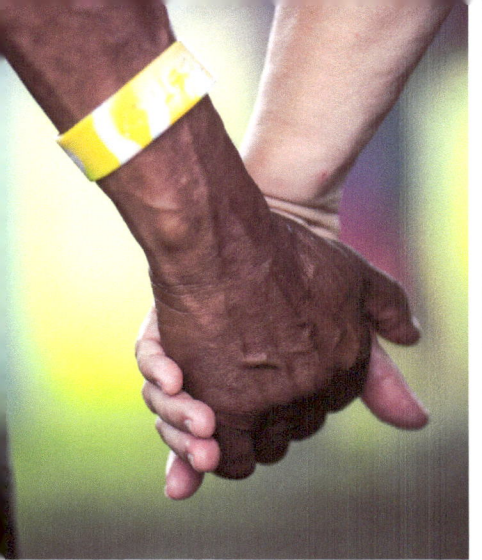

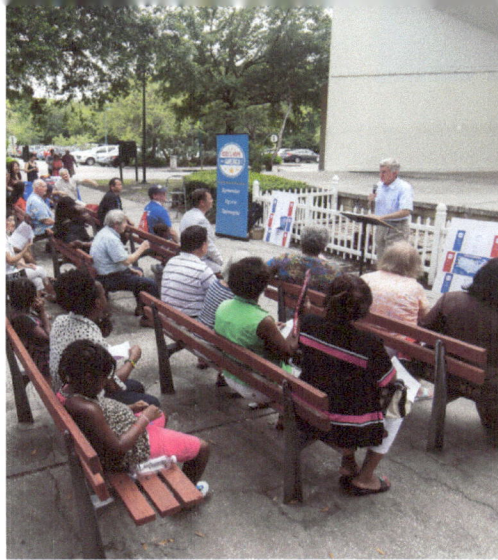

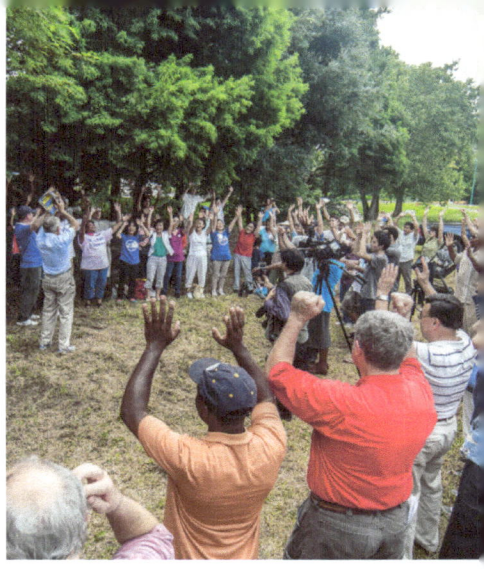

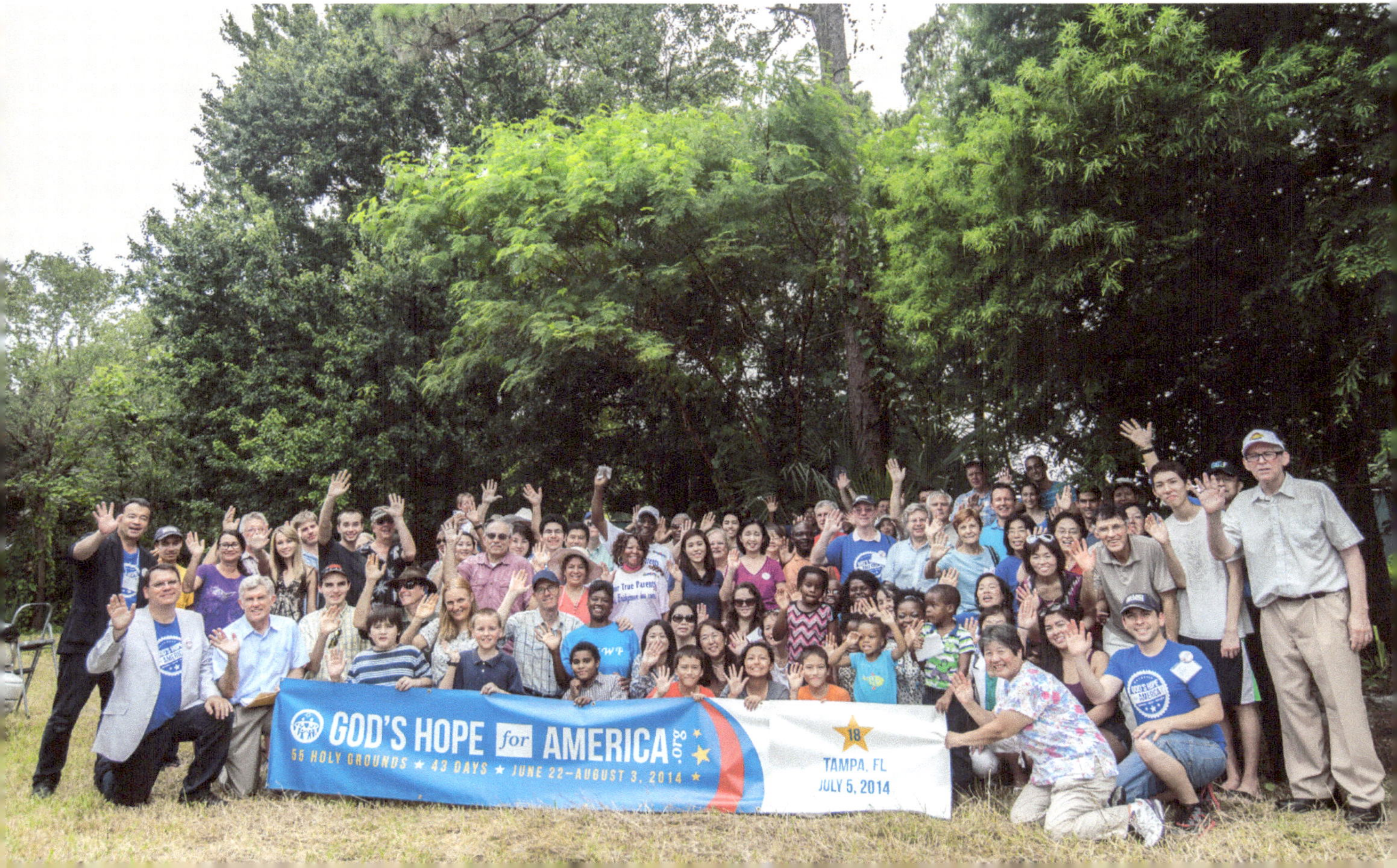

GOD'S HOPE for AMERICA.org
55 HOLY GROUNDS ★ 43 DAYS ★ JUNE 22–AUGUST 3, 2014
18
TAMPA, FL
JULY 5, 2014

MIAMI, FLORIDA

HOLY GROUND 19

EST: MARCH 8, 1965

GPS COORDINATES: 25°43'24.3"N 80°19'27.9"W

LOCATION

The Miami Holy Ground was originally located in a municipal park in Miami Beach but has since been re-located to Tropical Park in Miami. It is marked by a tree on the right side of a pathway between a parking lot and the only raised area of the park.

JOURNAL ENTRY

They traveled down the west coast of Florida to Miami Beach, where Rev. Moon blessed a beautiful site of soft green turf and swaying palm trees. There he dipped his finger into the smooth, gentle and warm waters of the Atlantic Ocean and, in Korean, wrote in the sand, "Abogee" (father) and "Omonee" (mother). The next morning they toured the town of Key West. Rev. Moon again dipped his finger in the waters of the southernmost beach in the United States. "America has so many different kinds of places," he remarked. "It's like many different countries rolled into one."

TROPICAL PARK
7900 SW 40 St.,
Miami, FL 33155

To Mrs. Moon

After coming from the west to the east, we will be heading north. While touring this large continent and selecting Holy Grounds in each state, I am hoping for the future development of America. When I first met the American members, there were many things that left an impression on me.

-Rev. Moon, March 14, 1965, Washington, D.C.

GATEWAY

The Gulf of Mexico is one of the great bodies of water in the United States. The God's Hope for America Pilgrimage offered a prayer of gratitude. just as the sun was setting and a storm brewed overhead.

SAVANNAH, GEORGIA

HOLY GROUND 20

EST: MARCH 10, 1965
GPS COORDINATES: 32°04'10.74" N 81°05'46.08" W

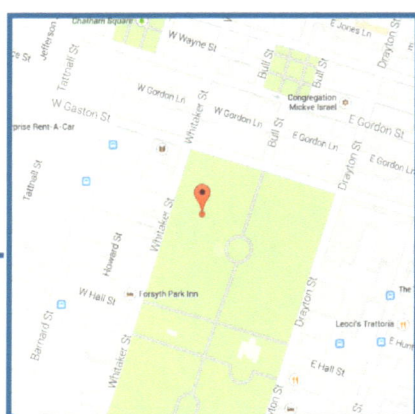

FORSYTH PARK
513 Whitaker St.,
Savannah, GA 31401

LOCATION

The Savannah Holy Ground is located in Forsyth Park. It lies northwest of a large, white fountain near the intersection of W. Huntingdon and Whitaker Streets. The Holy Ground is marked by a large oak tree with a split at the bottom of the trunk.

JOURNAL ENTRY

The time came to point the car north. After a day on the east coast of Florida, they were introduced to the red clay soil and pink magnolias of Georgia. In a beautifully flowering park in Savannah, among some strong oak trees, a Holy Ground was blessed.

To Mrs. Moon

As I experience all of these things, I think about how sorry I am that you could not come with me. However, I know that it will be better if you come after I pave the way, and I am grateful for everything, as this is the way of the Will.

-Rev. Moon, March 14, 1965, Washington, D.C.

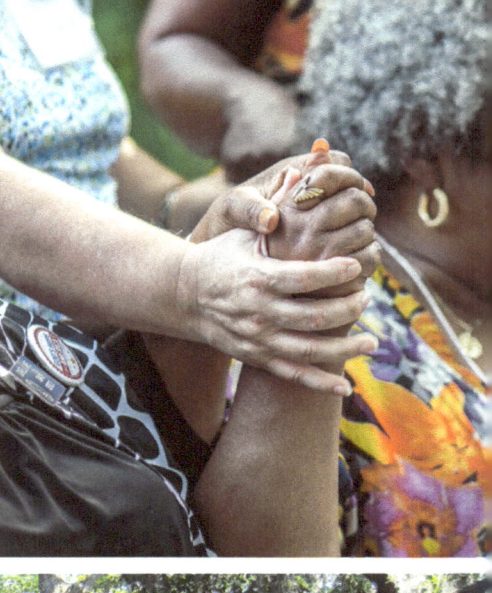

CAPITAL

During the God's Hope for America Pilgrimage, we hiked up Stone Mountain near Atlanta, Georgia, site of the founding of the second Ku Klux Klan in 1915 and location where secret rituals and meetings were once held. At the top, we prayed for forgiveness and repentance for the extreme suffering endured in this state. The mountain itself is beautiful, in spite of its sad history.

CAPITAL
OF CHANGE

REGION

TRAVEL TIME: MARCH 11, 1965 - MARCH 14, 1965

From Stone Mountain near Atlanta, GA, to Washington, D.C., the nation's capital, Holy Ground pilgrims will feel the historical significance of America as the tour transitions to America's thirteen original colonies.

"I am sure that the faith of the Pilgrim Fathers touched the heart of God. … God determined to give these faithful people the ultimate thing they wanted—freedom of worship. He then determined to give them even more."

—Rev. Moon, "God's Hope for America," Washington, D.C. October 21, 1973

CAPITAL

CHECKLIST OF HOLY GROUNDS

- ☐ Columbia, SC
- ☐ Raleigh, NC
- ☐ Richmond, VA
- ☐ Martinsburg, WV
- ☐ Washington, D.C.

COLUMBIA, S. CAROLINA

HOLY GROUND 21

EST: MARCH 11, 1965
GPS COORDINATES: 34°1'30" N 81°2'40" W

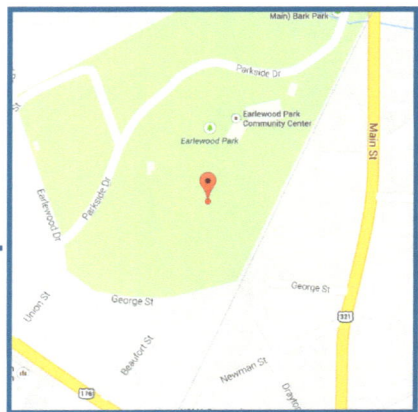

EARLEWOOD PARK
1111 Parkside Dr.,
Columbia, SC 29201

LOCATION

The Columbia Holy Ground is located in Earlewood Park. It is marked by a tall, straight pine tree near the center of the park, across from a water fountain. South Carolina claims home to four signers of the Declaration of Independence.

JOURNAL ENTRY

There were no Unificationists in Columbia, South Carolina. They drove through this area and moved on quickly. Rev. Moon made this stop on the original Holy Ground tour on March 11, 1965.

To Mrs. Moon

I pray that this can be a productive period, during which we can be filial before the Will and be examples for others. I know you are working hard to take of the children, but I have hope that you are preparing for the future with patience and gratitude.

-Rev. Moon, March 14, 1965, Washington, D.C.

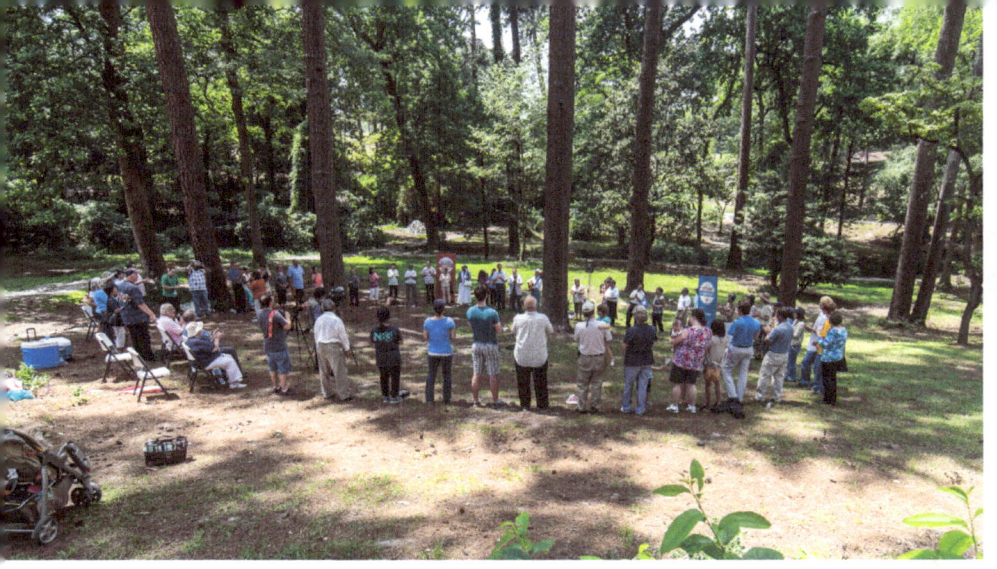

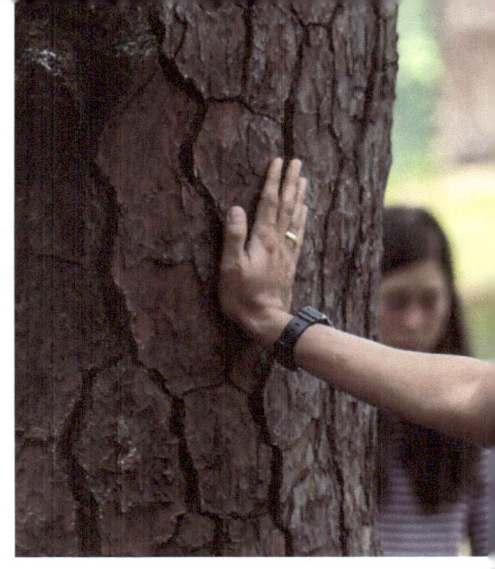

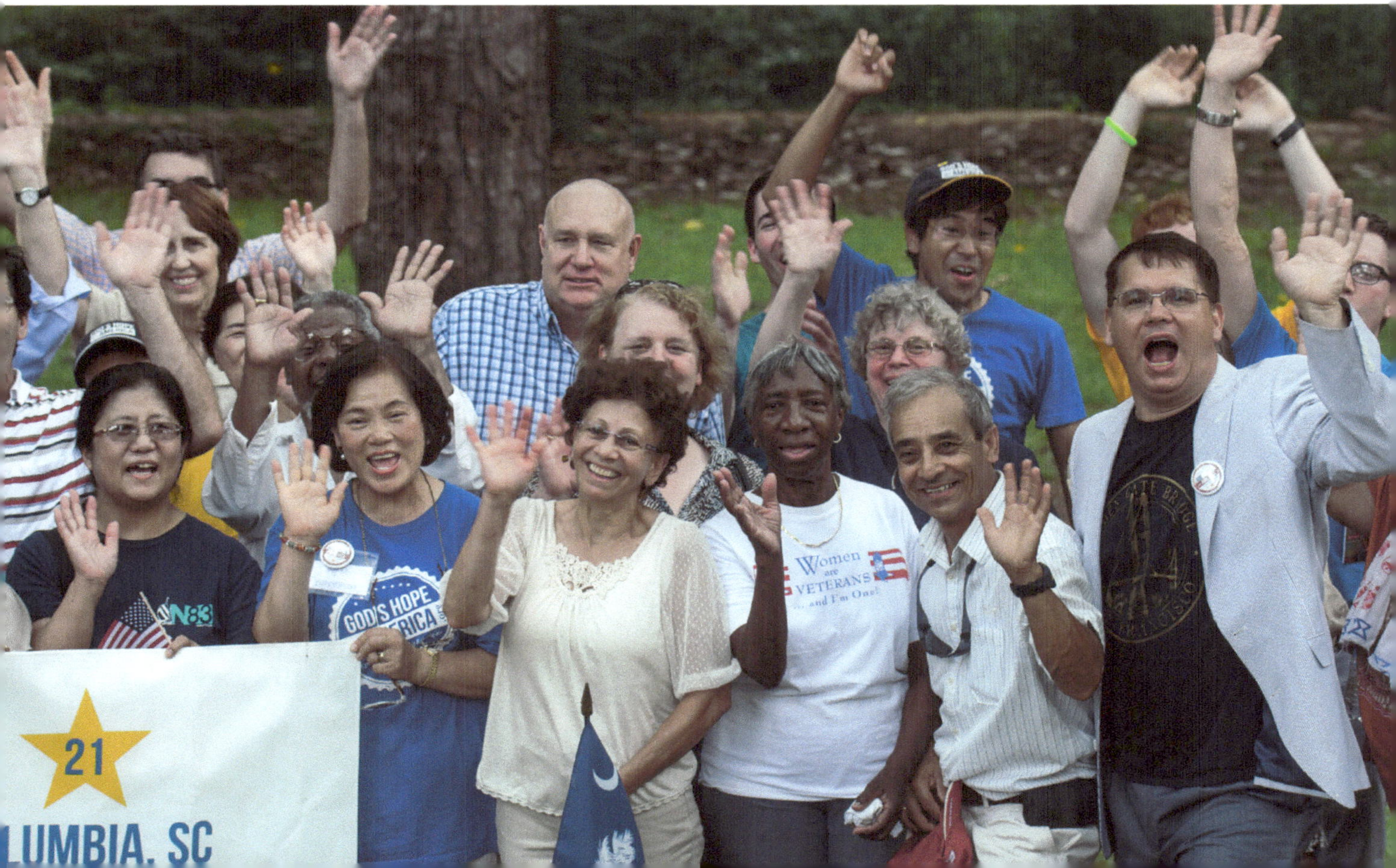
21
LUMBIA, SC
Women are VETERANS

RALEIGH,
N. CAROLINA

HOLY GROUND ⭐ 22

EST: MARCH 11, 1965
GPS COORDINATES: 35°46'11" N 78°39'2" W

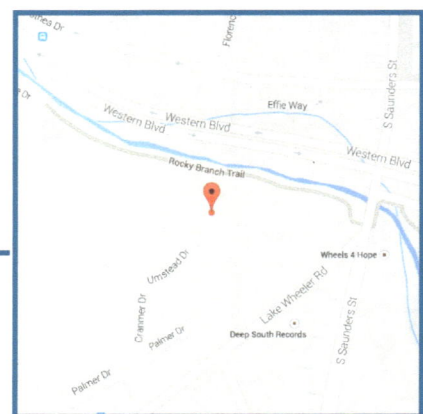

DOROTHEA DIX PARK
Umstead Dr.,
Raleigh, NC 27603

LOCATION

The Raleigh Holy Ground is located in Dorothea Dix Park. It was marked by a tree which is now gone. The exact location of the Holy Ground is therefore unknown. Raleigh might as well be called Museum City...there are museums for all ages and interests there! Check out the natural science museum, the history museum, the kids' museum or museum of art.

JOURNAL ENTRY

There were no Unificationists in Raleigh, North Carolina, either. They drove through this stretch and made their way to historic Richmond, Virginia.

To Mrs. Moon

The American members are also very high-spirited. I feel that the members at headquarters are working hard to fulfill their responsibilities.

-Rev. Moon, March 14, 1965, Washington, D.C.

RICHMOND, VIRGINIA

HOLY GROUND 23

EST: MARCH 11, 1965
GPS COORDINATES: 37°32'50" N 77°27'2" W

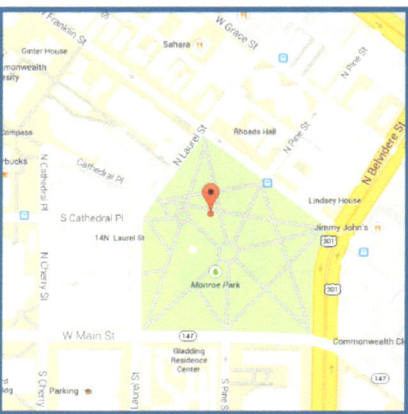

MONROE PARK
620 W Main St.,
Richmond, VA 23220

LOCATION

The Richmond Holy Ground is located in Monroe Park. It is in a grassy area between a fountain and a church with twin steeples on Laurel St. The Holy Ground is marked by the smallest tree in a group of large trees in this grassy area.

JOURNAL ENTRY

On March 11, after blessing a Holy Ground in Columbia, South Carolina, and Raleigh, North Carolina, they journeyed to Richmond, Virginia, where they visited a memorial dedicated to those from Virginia who had lost their lives in World War II and the Korean War. Leaving Richmond after blessing a Holy Ground there, they traveled to Fredericksburg, Virginia, and stayed overnight.

HELPFUL TIPS

- The Richmond Holy Ground is often used by a group of local Christians as their witnessing ground. If you happen to meet them, take the chance to get to know them, engage in interfaith dialogue and ask them what they think about God's Hope for America!

MARTINSBURG, W. VIRGINIA

HOLY GROUND 24

EST: MARCH 12, 1965
GPS COORDINATES: 39°28'3" N 77°58'50" W

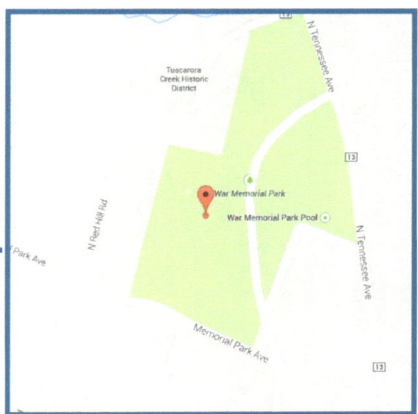

BERKELEY COUNTY WAR MEMORIAL PARK
500 N Tennessee Ave.,
Martinsburg, WV 25401

LOCATION

The Martinsburg Holy Ground is located in the Berkeley County War Memorial Park, off North Tennessee Ave. It is near two small buildings with green and white roofs. The Holy Ground is marked by a small tree that is sixth in a row, south of a line of bushes that run from east to west.

JOURNAL ENTRY

On March 12 the group passed through the Allegheny Mountains and arrived in Martinsburg, West Virginia. At the Windewald Motel south of the city limits, some Unificationists from Washington, D.C., greeted Rev. Moon and accompanied them to the Holy Ground site, in a small valley among some young trees.

DID YOU KNOW?

- The Moons loved West Virginia. They often landed at the nearby airport and spent time at a hunting lodge in the mountains to meditate and enjoy nature.

- "Take Me Home, Country Roads" became the state anthem in March 2014. It describes West Virginia as being "Almost Heaven."

WASHINGTON, D.C.

HOLY GROUND 25

EST: MARCH 14, 1965
GPS COORDINATES: 38°53'24" N 77°0'41" W

LOCATION

The Washington, D.C., Capitol Building Holy Ground is marked by the central evergreen tree on the lawn west of the Capitol Building. It was a site chosen by Rev. Moon to remind America's leaders to pray before making important decisions.

JOURNAL ENTRY

Next, they went over to the U.S. Capitol for a picnic lunch. With the great white dome of the Capitol looming before them and the Washington Monument piercing the sky behind, they stood around a fir tree and Rev. Moon blessed the Holy Ground. [That fir tree is now gone.] They closed by praying fervently for the United States. Suddenly the chimes from a nearby carillon began pealing, "God Bless America." They smiled at each other with tears in their eyes and knew this moment belonged to their Heavenly Parent.

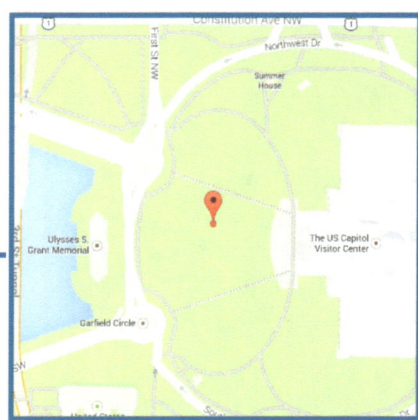

UNITED STATES CAPITOL WEST LAWN
First St. SE,
Washington, D.C. 20004

To Mrs. Moon

I am writing you from the capital of the United States. One month has passed and … I never before experienced such huge changes between the environment and climate of one location and the next as I have in the course of this tour.

-Rev. Moon, March 14, 1965, Washington, D.C.

WASHINGTON, D.C.

HOLY GROUND

EST: MARCH 14, 1965
GPS COORDINATES: 38°53'39" N 77°2'12" W

LOCATION

The Washington, D.C., White House Holy Ground is located in the direct center of the Ellipse, an oval field directly south of the White House. Most museums and historical sites in D.C. are free! Among the best are the National Archives, the Natural History Museum, the Air and Space Museum and the Native American History Museum. If you happen to be there on July 4th, the Capitol lawn is an excellent place to view the fireworks.

JOURNAL ENTRY

As the holy procession came down from the hills of West Virginia and into the nation's capital, they marveled at the massive white government buildings and memorials and the great, grassy National Mall. First they went to the Ellipse behind the White House. With the White House before them and the Washington Monument behind them, Rev. Moon blessed the Holy Ground.

WHITE HOUSE ELLIPSE
1600 Pennsylvania Ave. NW, Washington, D.C.

To Mrs. Moon

As of today, I have selected 21 Holy Grounds, including the one in Washington, D.C., that I established this morning at 11:00 a.m. You will be able to see pictures of all the Holy Grounds later.

-Rev. Moon, March 14, 1965, Washington, D.C.

ATLANTIC
THE HISTORY

REGION D

TRAVEL TIME: MARCH 15, 1965 - MARCH 20, 1965

Much of America's formational history can be experienced on the Atlantic tour, which takes you deeper into the original thirteen colonies. Visit Gettysburg, the 9/11 Memorial Museum, Plymouth Rock and sites important to Rev. and Mrs. Moon.

"The story of the American Pilgrim Fathers is one of a kind in God's history. … These Pilgrims were the Abrahams of modern history."

—Rev. Moon, "God's Hope for America," Washington, D.C. October 21, 1973

D ATLANTIC

CHECKLIST OF HOLY GROUNDS

- ☐ Baltimore, MD
- ☐ Wilmington, DE
- ☐ Philadelphia, PA
- ☐ Trenton, NJ
- ☐ New York City, NY
- ☐ New Haven, CT
- ☐ Providence, RI
- ☐ Boston, MA
- ☐ Portsmouth, NH
- ☐ Kittery, ME
- ☐ Brattleboro, VT

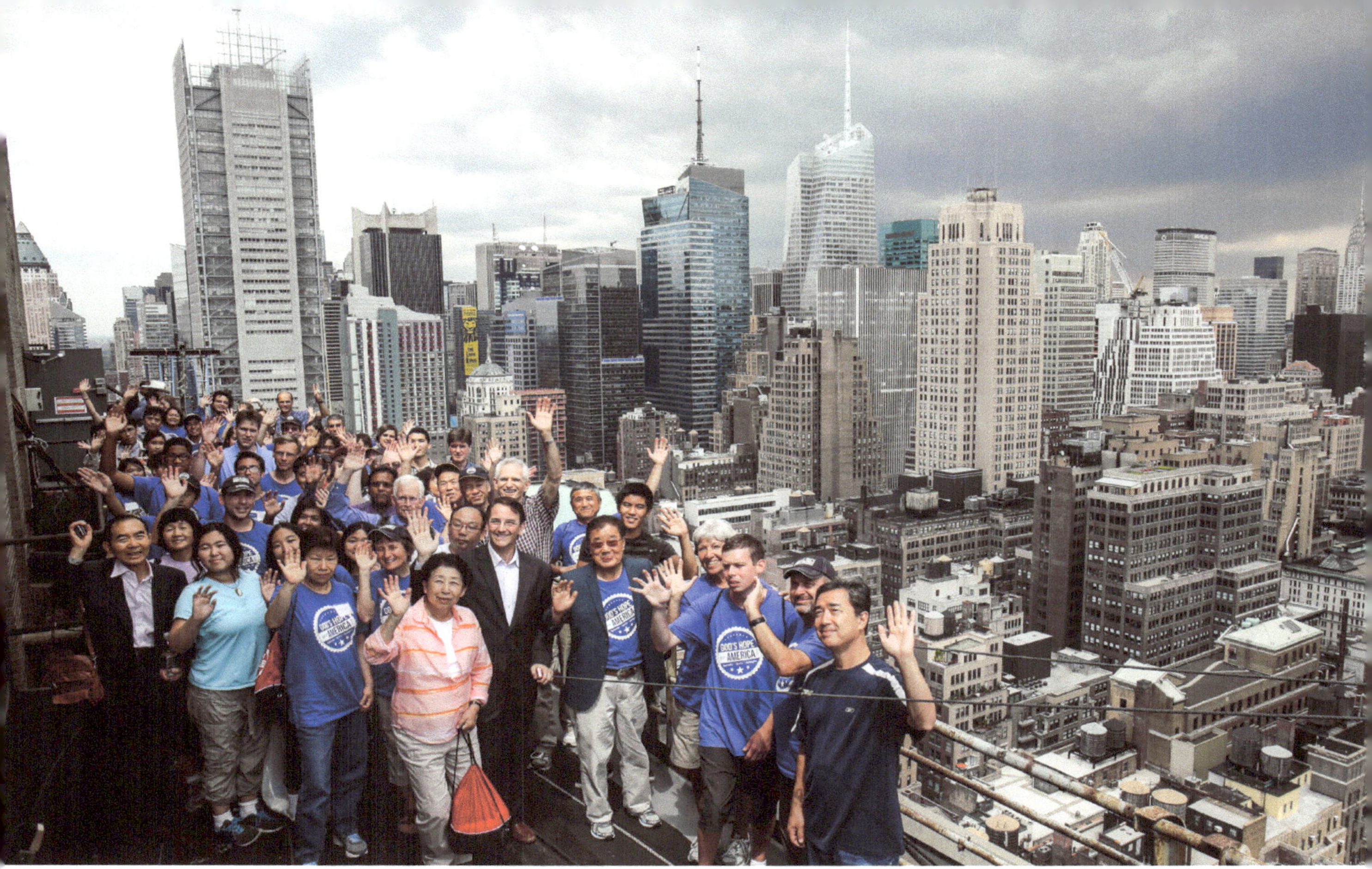

UNIVERSITY OF
BRIDGEPORT
MCM
XXVII

JARDIM

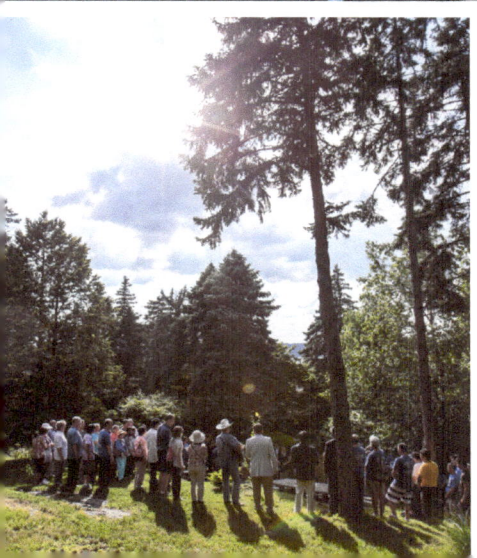

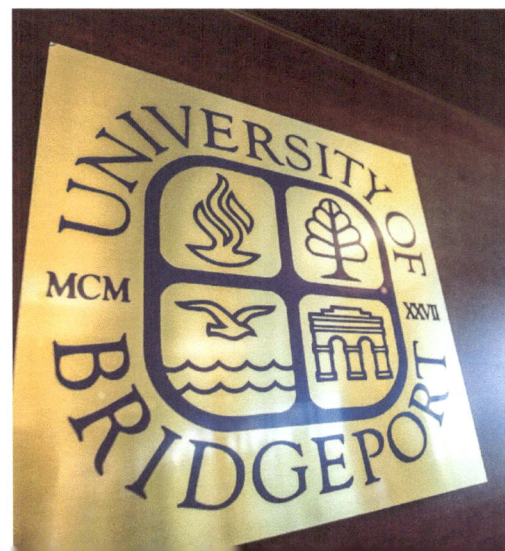

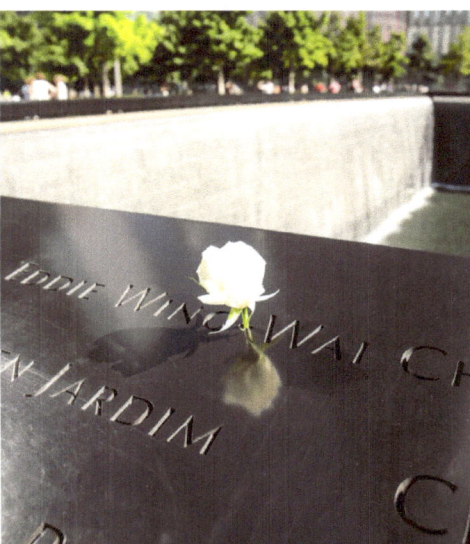

BALTIMORE, MARYLAND

HOLY GROUND 27

EST: MARCH 15, 1965
GPS COORDINATES: 39°19'25" N 76°38'40" W

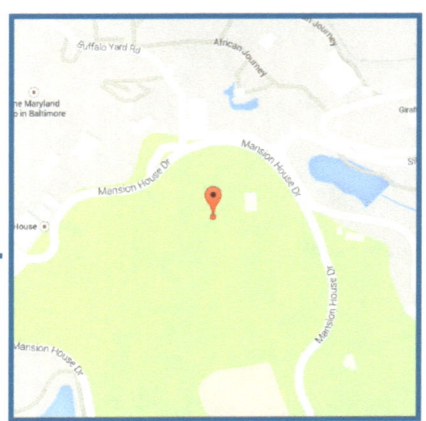

DRUID HILL PARK
5 Terrace Dale,
Towson, MD 21286

LOCATION

The Baltimore Holy Ground is located in Druid Hill Park surrounded by rolling hills and streams. The original trees of the Holy Ground have been replaced with three new trees. The Holy Ground was originally marked by a large tree near the top of the hill between a park administration building and a duck pond. That tree has since been replaced by a new smaller tree, near the current police station.

JOURNAL ENTRY

Their next stop was Baltimore, famous for its white marble steps, in the state of Maryland. There, Rev. Moon blessed a Holy Ground for that state.

To Mrs. Moon

I received your letter the other day in Washington, D.C. I felt indescribable joy upon receiving your letter. I realize how important it is to communicate with you while we are apart.

-Rev. Moon, March 20, 1965, Brattleboro, VT

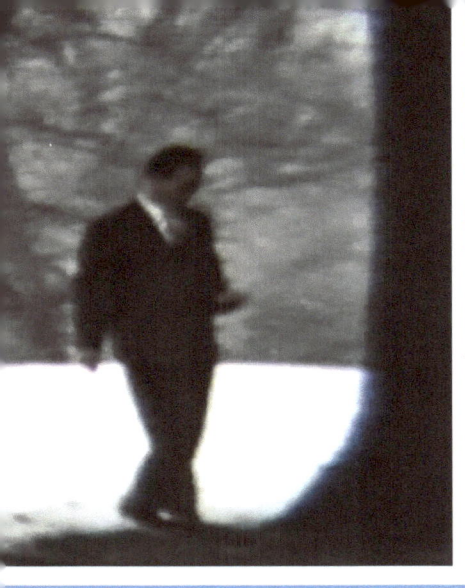

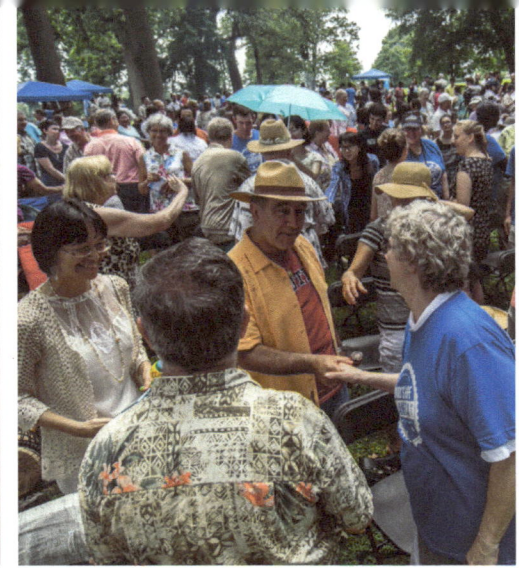

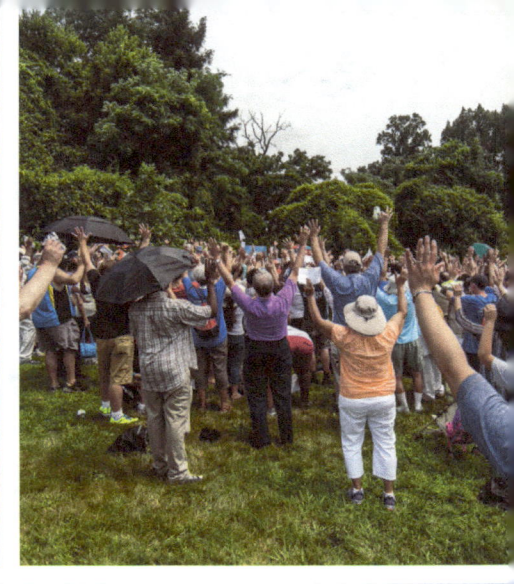

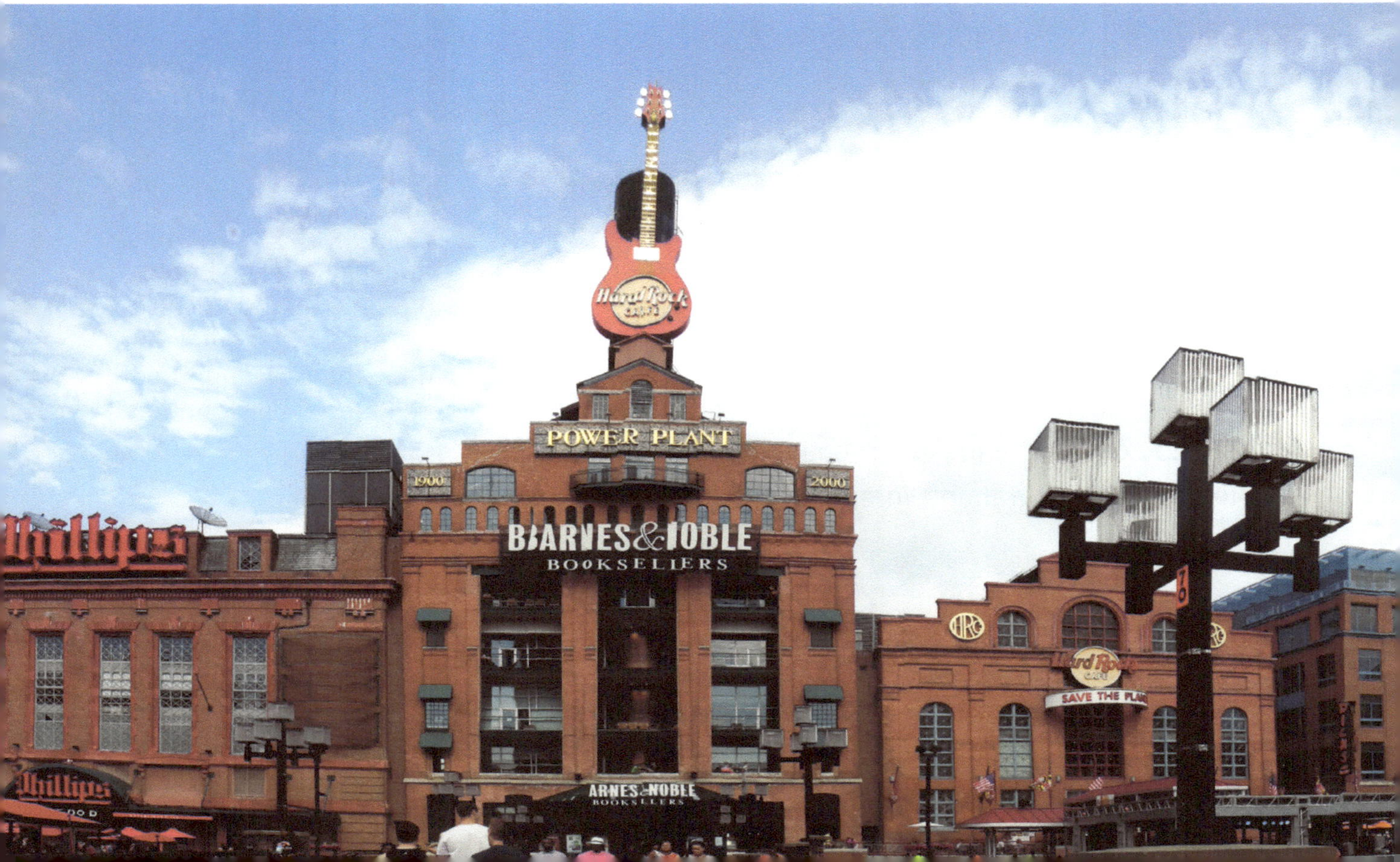
POWER PLANT
1900
2000
BOOKSELLERS

WILMINGTON, DELAWARE

HOLY GROUND 28

EST: MARCH 15, 1965
GPS COORDINATES: 39°45'19" N 75°32'59" W

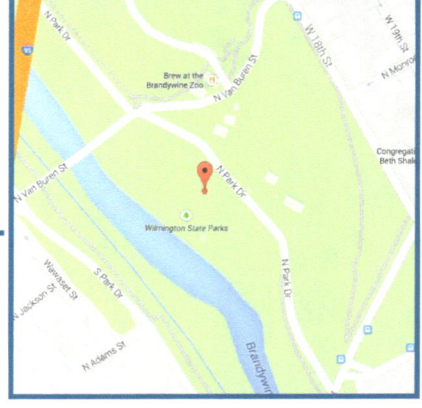

BRANDYWINE PARK
Near the corner of N. Van Buren St. and Stadium Dr., Wilmington, DE 19802

LOCATION

The Wilmington Holy Ground is located in Brandywine Park, near N. Van Buren Street and N Park Drive. It is marked by a large tree in a small glen southwest of a sports field. Wilmington is central to a potential day trip into Pennsylvania that's rich in history. Stop by Gettysburg and say a prayer at the soldiers' cemetery, visit Valley Forge, and spend some time in Amish country for an interesting and immersive cultural and interfaith experience.

JOURNAL ENTRY

After Baltimore was Wilmington, in the even tinier state of Delaware, where city blocks are called "squares" and the favorite sport is boating. Rev. Moon blessed a Holy Ground there as well.

To Mrs. Moon

While we are separated like this, although each of us has to take care of many things, I feel that a greater power is bonding us together even more strongly. Therefore, I hope that you, Omma, will experience how precious and great it is to have endured when you look back on this experience.

-Rev. Moon, March 20, 1965, Brattleboro, VT

GOD'S HOPE for AMERICA
GOD'S HOPE for AMERICA
JULY 15, 2014

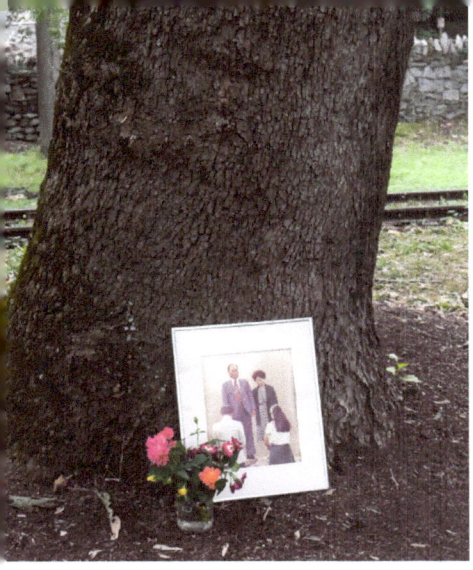

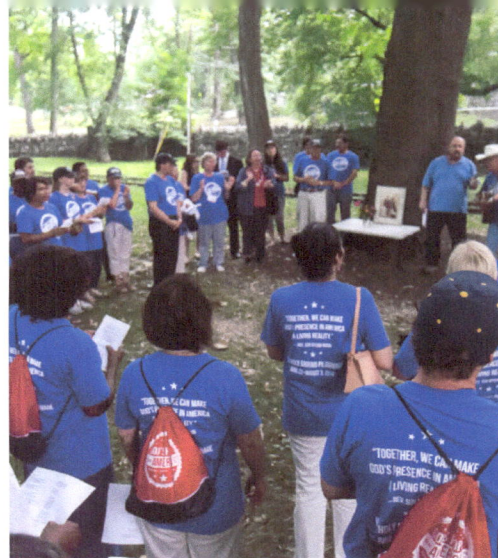

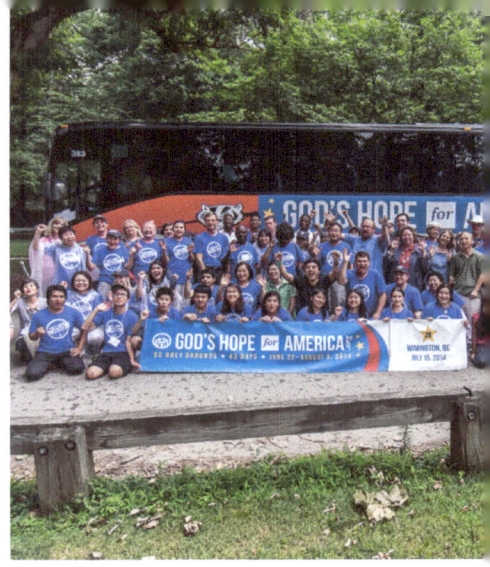

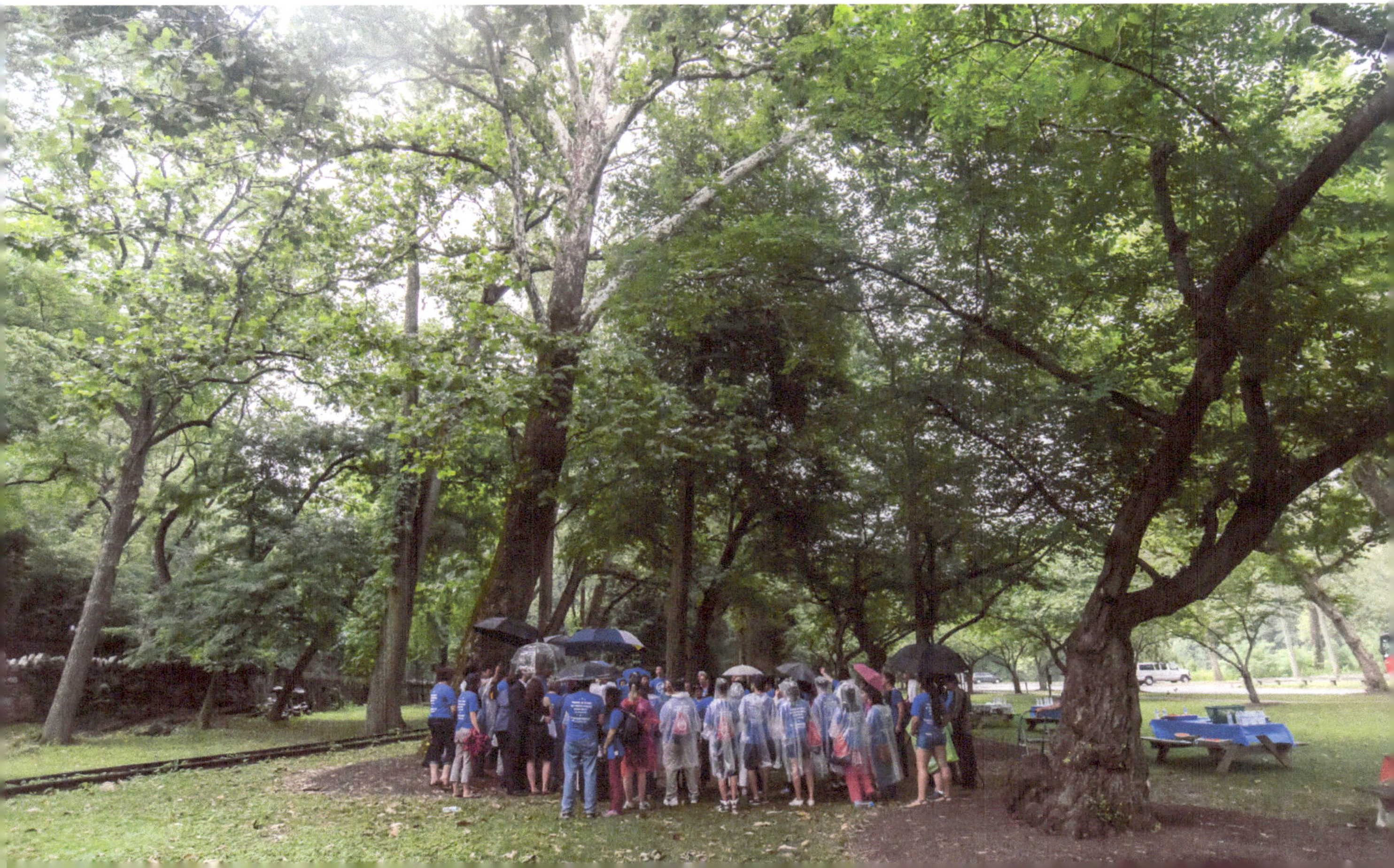

PHILADELPHIA, PENNSYLVANIA

HOLY GROUND 29

EST: MARCH 16, 1965
GPS COORDINATES: 39°58'36" N 75°12'23" W

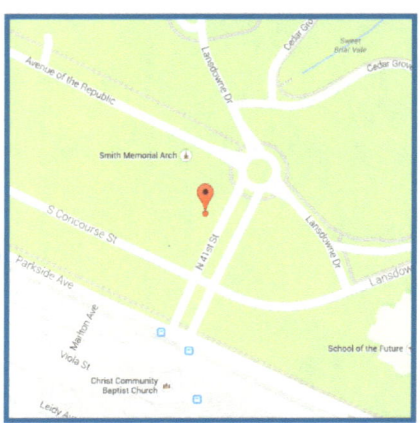

W. FAIRMOUNT PARK
1250-1258 N 41st St.,
Philadelphia, PA 19121

LOCATION

The Philadelphia Holy Ground is in Fairmount Park, located in a field southeast of the park's main gate. It is marked by a large tree between the main gate and the street opposite. The Founding Fathers of the United States wrote the Declaration of Independence and Constitution in Philadelphia. They echo God's hopes for America.

JOURNAL ENTRY

The next city to receive Rev. Moon's blessing was Philadelphia, Pennsylvania. There the group stayed several hours to visit Arthur Ford, a well-known trance medium, whose spirit guide said, "The light around you [all of them in the room] is so bright that it would blind most of you. … In other circumstances, my instrument [Arthur Ford] and you should take off your shoes. You are sitting in the presence of Truth incarnate!"

To Mrs. Moon

In this world in which we are living, I again realize how important it is to march forward toward victory, shedding tears as we fulfill our great responsibility and mission.

-Rev. Moon, March 20, 1965, Brattleboro, VT

ATLANTIC

On July 14, the God's Hope for America Holy Ground pilgrimage paid homage at one of America's most sacred, hallowed sites, the battlefield at Gettysburg, PA. It was here, over the course of three sweltering days in the summer of 1863, that the tide of the Civil War turned once and for all. The price paid on both sides was appallingly high—almost 50,000 casualties in just three days.

TRENTON, NEW JERSEY

HOLY GROUND 30

EST: MARCH 17, 1965
GPS COORDINATES: 40°14'13" N 74°47'18" W

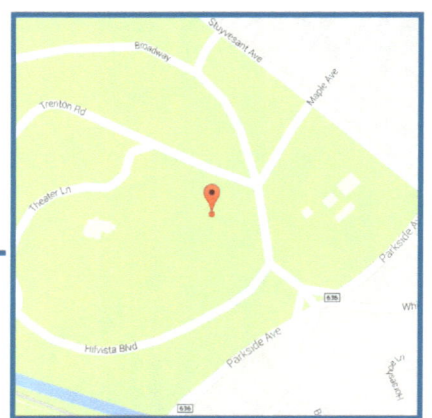

CADWALADER PARK
229 Parkside Ave.,
Trenton, NJ 08608

LOCATION

The Trenton Holy Ground is located in Cadwalader Park, at Parkside Ave. and the Trenton City Museum. The Holy Ground is marked by a tree near a bear cage and the large Gettysburg Appomattox statue. This park houses the Trenton City Museum, with exhibits on the history of Native American life in this region. The Elizabeth and Clifton New Jersey Family Church centers are just a short drive apart.

JOURNAL ENTRY

After blessing the Holy Ground in Philadelphia, they turned along the New Jersey Turnpike to Trenton, capital of New Jersey, and arrived at the Holy Ground site in the evening.

To Mrs. Moon

I feel I have so much to be grateful to you for. All that we do is for the sake of the Will, which is so great and high, and the work we will have to do is in proportion to that. So let us keep going forward.

-Rev. Moon, March 20, 1965, Brattleboro, VT

ERECTED
AS A TRIBUTE TO
LOYALTY PATRIOTISM
AND VALOR.

GOD'S HOPE for AMERICA
Remember
Revive
Reimagine
GOD'S HOPE for AMERICA
TRENTON, NJ
JULY 16, 2014
GOD'S HOPE for AMERICA
Remember
Revive
Reimagine

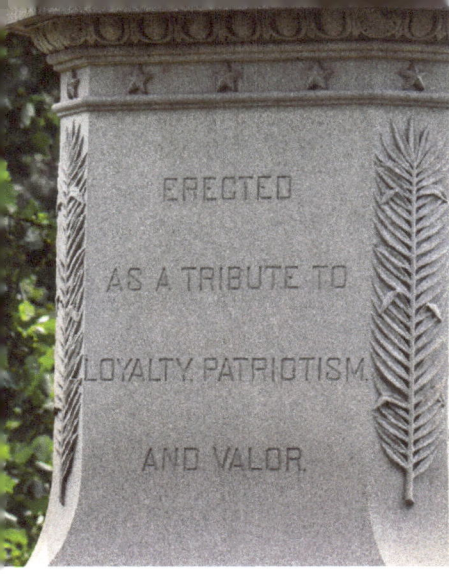

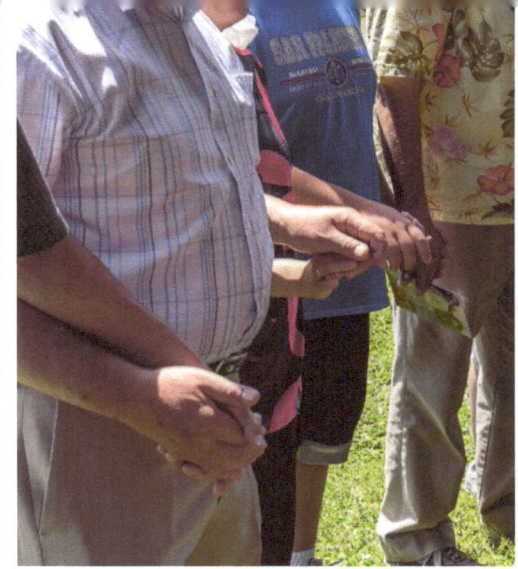

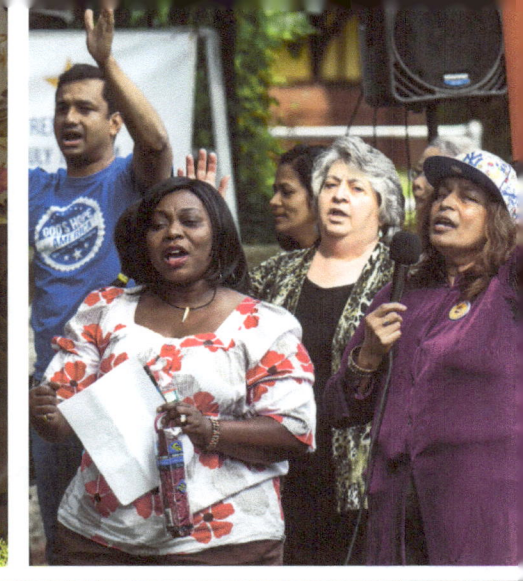

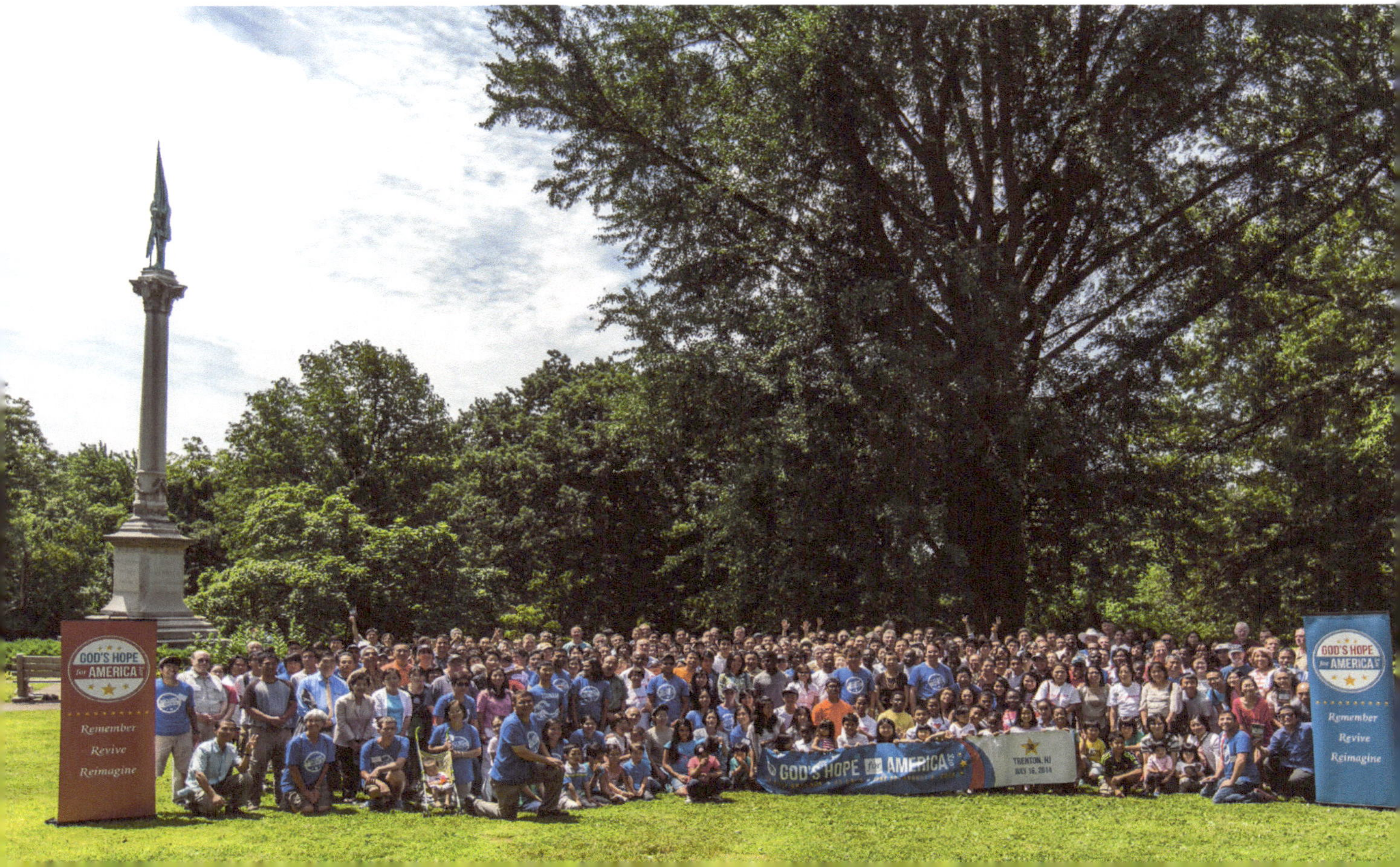

NEW YORK, NEW YORK

HOLY GROUND 31

EST: MARCH 19, 1965
GPS COORDINATES: 40°46'40" N 73°58'9" W

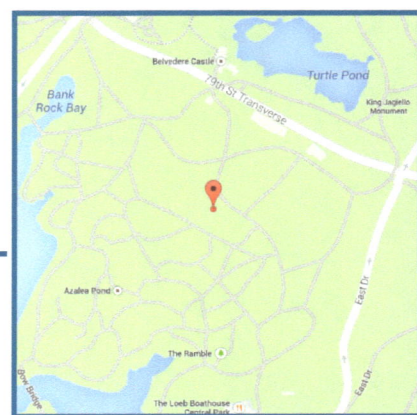

CENTRAL PARK
East 72nd Street
and 5th Ave.,
New York, NY 10591

LOCATION

The New York City Holy Ground is located in Central Park near 72nd St. It is west of the Central Park Boathouse, across a stream. It is marked by a large boulder twenty feet in width.

JOURNAL ENTRY

In the morning they went to Central Park where Rev. Moon decided upon a small tree growing out of a huge, flat rock. Among the towering grandeur and bustle, the entire Holy Ground was blessed on a rock measuring at least 20 feet across. The tree growing out of it was splitting the solid rock apart. "This shows the strength of even a small plant," Rev. Moon said. "You should be like this tree. ... You may feel small, but with the Divine Principle you have the tool to be powerful."

WHILE IN THE AREA

- Visit the 9/11 Memorial Museum

- Take the time to visit Belvedere, East Garden and the Unification Theological Seminary, three places where the Moons spent much of their time building their ministry in America.

BELVEDERE, NEW YORK

GPS COORDINATES: 41°03'02.7"N 73°51'48.0"W

BELVEDERE
723 South Broadway,
Tarrytown, NY 10591

MAIN EDUCATION CENTER

In the early years of the Unification Movement in America, the Belvedere Training Center in Tarrytown, New York, hosted many educational workshops for Unificationists. Rev. Moon personally spoke at length on God's hope for America and on the responsibility of America towards God and the world. Celebrations and Holy Days were observed here before East Garden became the central place of ministry in the United States. The God's Hope for America Pilgrimage stopped here to pray at the Holy Rock.

Belvedere is located just half a mile down the road from East Garden. The grounds are currently used as a place for worship, youth-related activities and evening educational programs.

To Mrs. Moon

While I travel, I am dreaming about a tomorrow that will be filled with hope and the world stage that we will reach together. I rejoice thinking of the days to come when we will embark on speaking tours together.

-Rev. Moon, March 20, 1965, Brattleboro, VT

EAST GARDEN, NEW YORK

GPS COORDINATES: 41°02'53.4"N 73°51'25.3"W

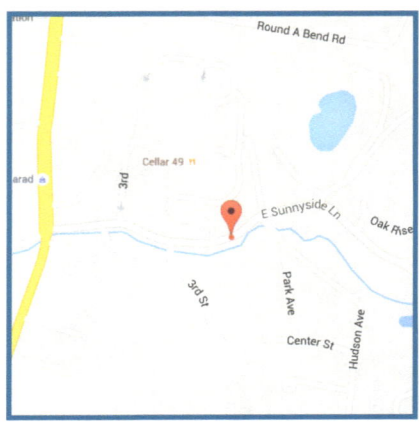

EAST GARDEN
50 East Sunnyside Lane,
Irvington, NY 10533

REV. AND MRS. MOON'S MINISTRY

Though East Garden was not one of the original Holy Grounds established in 1965, it was the Moons' central place of ministry in the United States for more than 30 years. The God's Hope for America Pilgrimage made a special stop at Father's Prayer Rock. Rev. Moon had offered so many tearful prayers of his own at this site. For many, it was their first time visiting this historic place. We took the time to soak in the atmosphere and tour the grounds.

East Garden is a large estate set in Irvington, New York. The grounds boast a beautiful Japanese rock garden, several structures and a newly installed museum, housing historic memorabilia of the Moons' time in America. The Holy Rock is opposite the rock garden, up a set of steps into a grove of trees. A bench where Rev. Moon often sat in the early hours of the morning to pray and meditate is set upon a large rock and marks the Holy Ground.

To Mrs. Moon

I yearn for the day when you will become the great True Mother who will bring victory over evil and fulfill all her responsibilities. Whenever I miss you and the children, I look at pictures of you and yearn for when I will see you again.

-Rev. Moon, March 20, 1965, Brattleboro, VT

GOD'S HOPE for AMERICA
NEW YORK CITY, NY
JULY 17, 2014

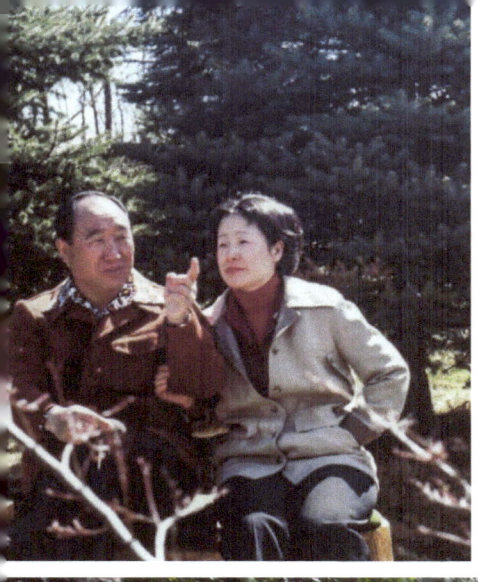

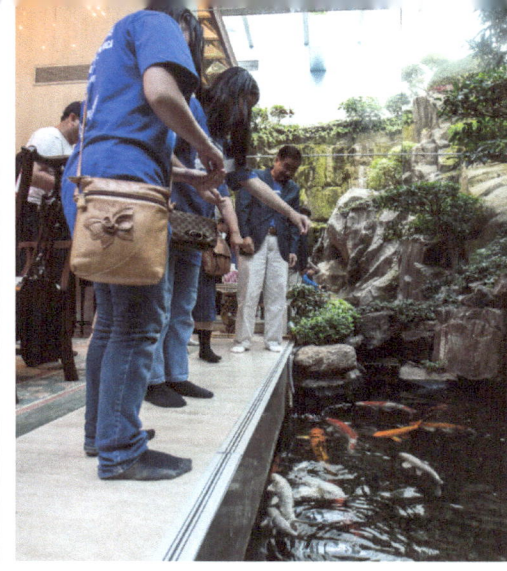

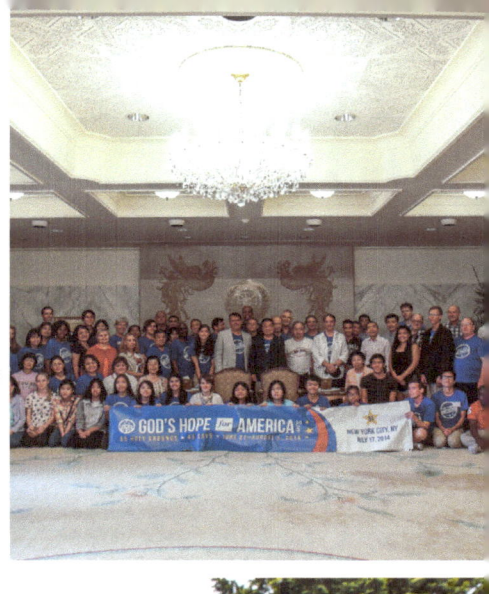

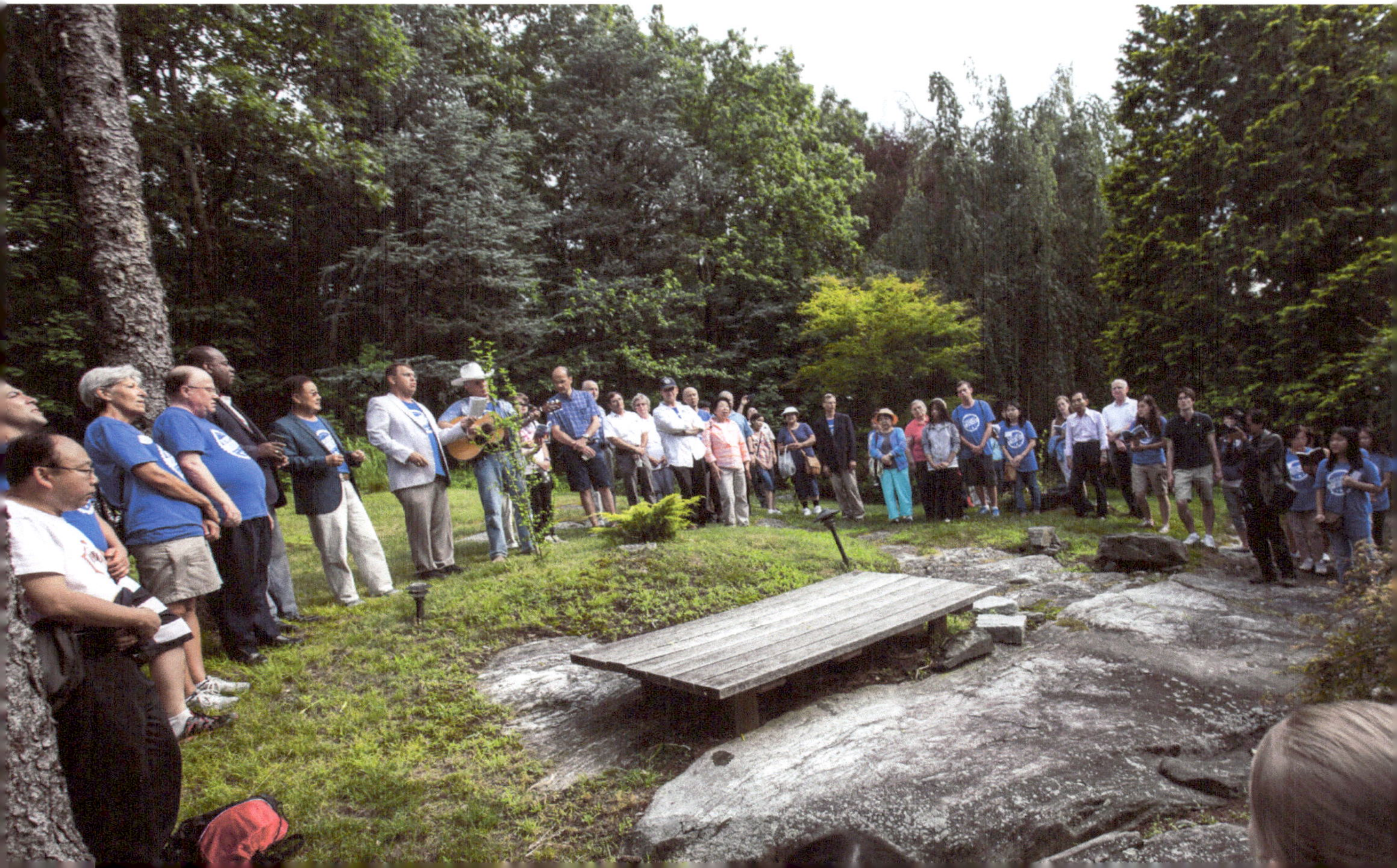

NEW HAVEN, CONNECTICUT

HOLY GROUND ⭐ 32

EST: MARCH 19, 1965
GPS COORDINATES: 41°19'57.5"N 72°57'44.6"W

WEST ROCK RIDGE STATE PARK
1110 Wintergreen Ave., New Haven, CT 06514

LOCATION

The New Haven Holy Ground is located in West Rock Ridge State Park. It can be found at the end of Baldwin Drive and is marked by a large, flat rock in the woods near a stone cottage at the top of a hill. The road winds down and then continues up. There is an overlook on the far side of the parking lot across from the Holy Ground—don't miss the spectacular view!

JOURNAL ENTRY

The farmland of Maryland, Delaware and New Jersey began to change to the typical woodlands of New England. They followed the twisting course of a small river through shady glens and forest groves of pine and birch until they reached the university town of New Haven, Connecticut. Rev. Moon blessed a Holy Ground, and they hurried north to Providence, Rhode Island, site of his next blessing.

HELPFUL TIPS

- Make time to drive past Danbury Prison, where Rev. Moon was unjustly incarcerated, and offer a prayer of healing. Then visit the University of Bridgeport, one of the schools Rev. Moon supported in America, on the way to your next stop.

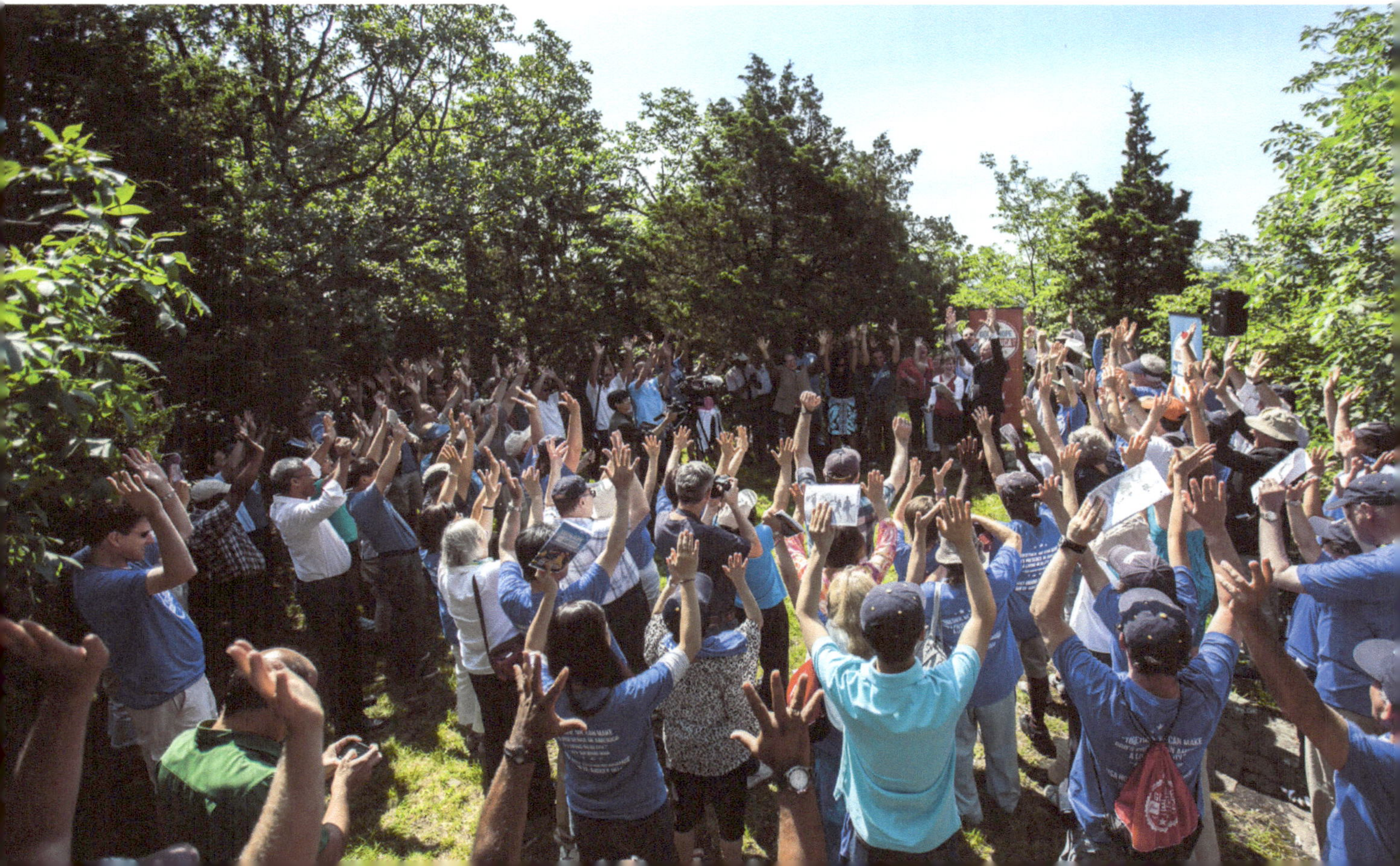

PROVIDENCE,
RHODE ISLAND

HOLY GROUND ⭐ 33

EST: MARCH 19, 1965
GPS COORDINATES: 41°47'10.7"N 71°24'30.4"W

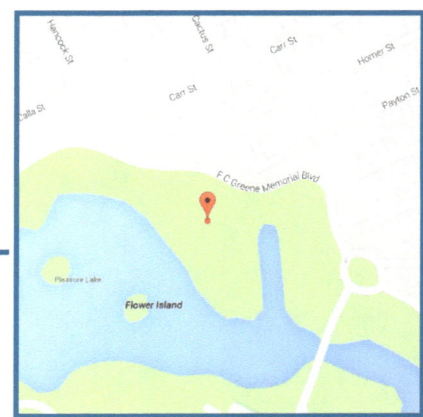

ROGER WILLIAMS PARK
136 Carr St.,
Providence, RI 02905

LOCATION

The Providence Holy Ground is located in Roger Williams Park, set between four tall pines and almost directly in the backyard of the church. Swans can be seen swimming in the serene lake beside the Holy Ground.

JOURNAL ENTRY

North they went to the church spires and peaceful villages of historic New England. The car whizzed through Connecticut, Rhode Island, the Public Garden of Boston, Massachusetts, and on to northern New Hampshire. In that single day, Rev. Moon blessed Holy Grounds in six states!

HELPFUL TIPS

- Providence is one of the oldest cities in the United States. It is home to the first Baptist church in the country, various historic buildings, and many remnants of the early years of this nation. Take time to explore while you're here!

BOSTON, MASSACHUSETTS

HOLY GROUND 34

EST: MARCH 19, 1965
GPS COORDINATES: 42°21'12.8"N 71°04'11.5"W

BOSTON COMMONS
9 Arlington St.,
Boston, MA 02116

LOCATION

The Holy Ground is located in Boston Commons, the oldest city park in America. It lies on a little peninsula on the Arlington Street side of the Swan Boat Pond, inside the Boston Public Garden. A stone footbridge crosses over the pond. With your back to the Boston Commons, walk down the stairs on the left side at the far end of the footbridge. Follow the edge of the pond to the first outcropping which includes a willow and a maple tree.

JOURNAL ENTRY

From Providence, they traveled on to Boston, Massachusetts, arriving at about 7 p.m. The citizens of that respectable city were nonplussed to see them in the Boston Public Garden praying and dedicating the land to God.

WHILE IN THE AREA

- Boston is rich with history. In fact, this Holy Ground is located where the story of America, and how it came to be the independent country it is today, began. Connect to the roots of this nation and visit the Paul Revere House, the Freedom Trail and the museums.

GOD'S HOPE
for AMERICA
NATIONAL TOUR
Remember · Revive · Reimagin
godshopeforamerica.org

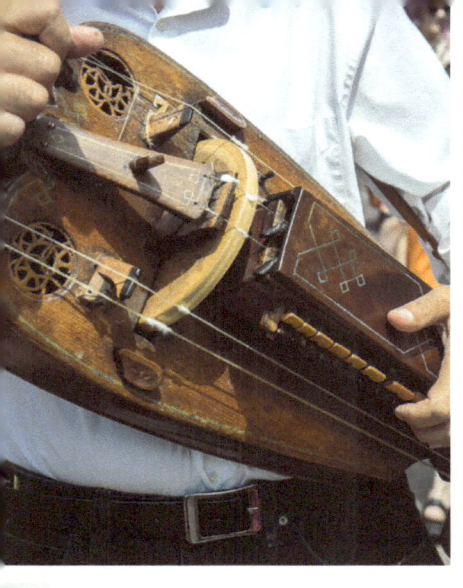

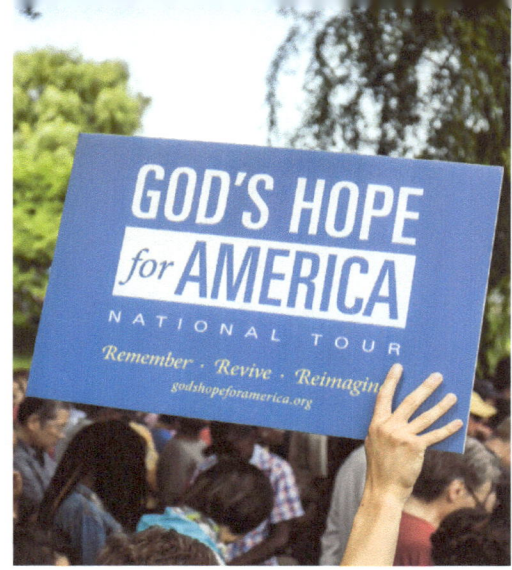

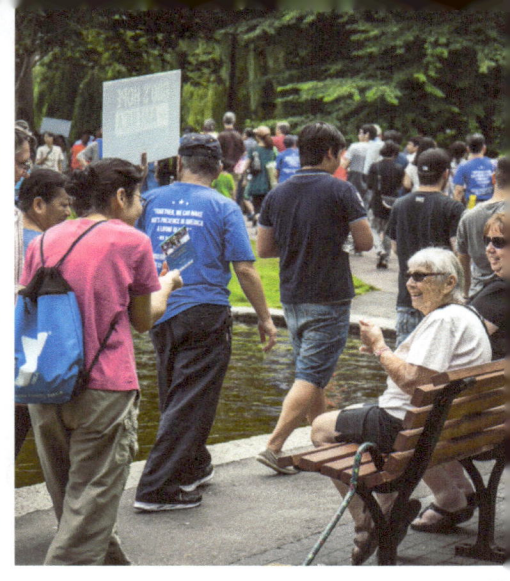

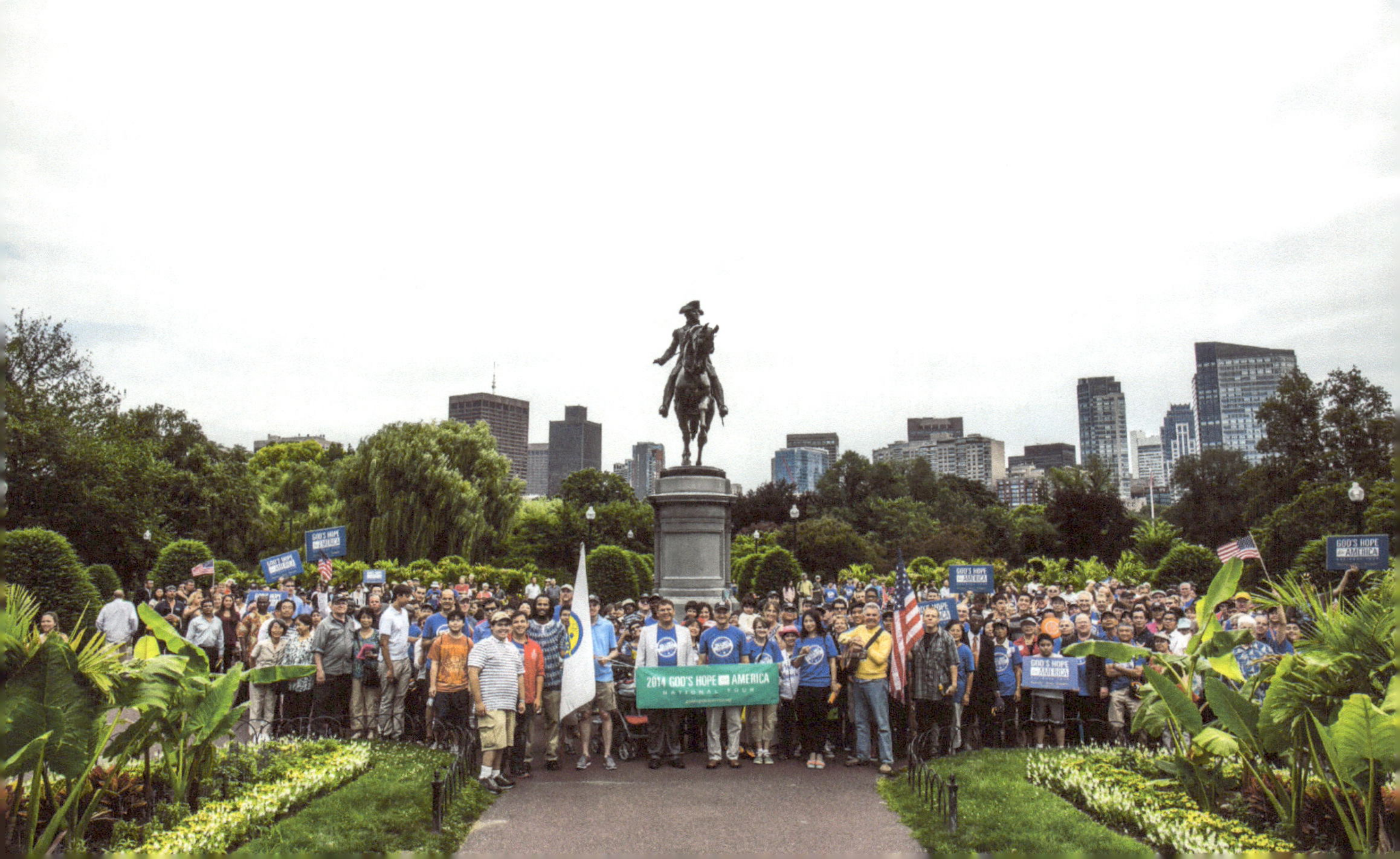
2014 GOD'S HOPE for AMERICA
NATIONAL TOUR

PORTSMOUTH, NEW HAMPSHIRE

HOLY GROUND 35

EST: MARCH 19, 1965
GPS COORDINATES: 43°04'24.3"N 70°45'54.3"W

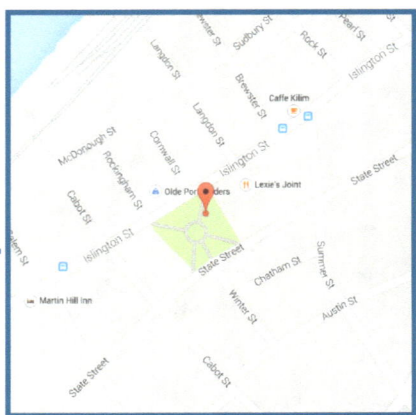

GOODWIN PARK
663 State St.,
Portsmouth, NH 03801

LOCATION

The Portsmouth Holy Ground is located in Goodwin Park, between Islington St. and State St. It is marked by a large evergreen tree northeast of a monument.

JOURNAL ENTRY

The traffic on the Eastern Seaboard is very heavy. People were really "on the go," and they didn't reach Portsmouth, New Hampshire, until 10 p.m. that evening. A full, yellow-orange moon shone down on Rev. Moon as he blessed the frozen ground in the city park.

To Mrs. Moon

I trust that you will do well, and that you will become the kind of woman who will be most precious to me, in whom I will take much pride as the woman of all women. When I think of this, I realize what a happy man I am! With this, I will move forward.

-Rev. Moon, March 20, 1965, Brattleboro, VT

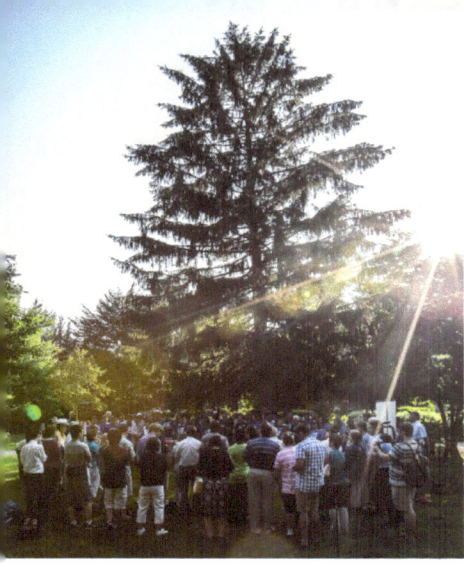

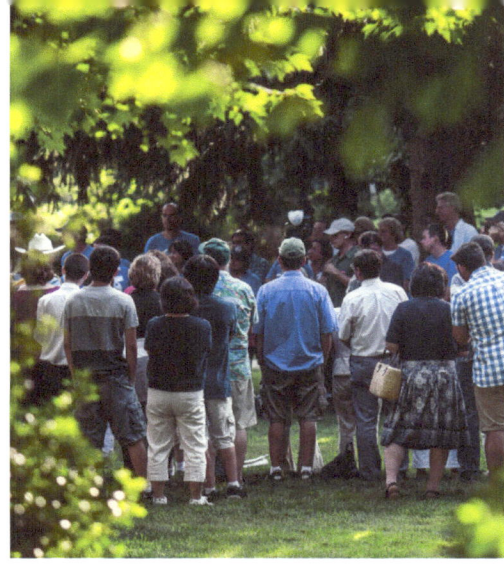

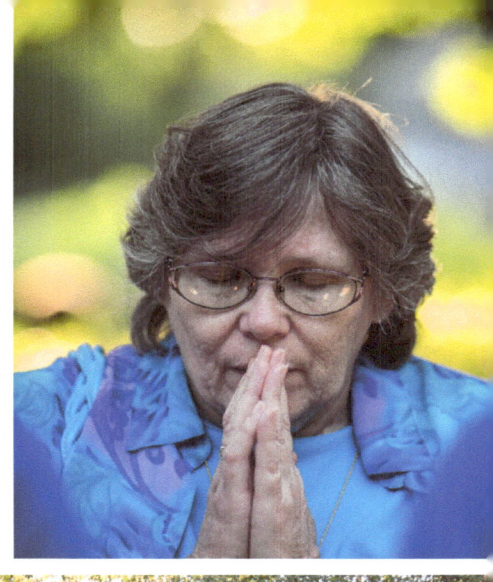

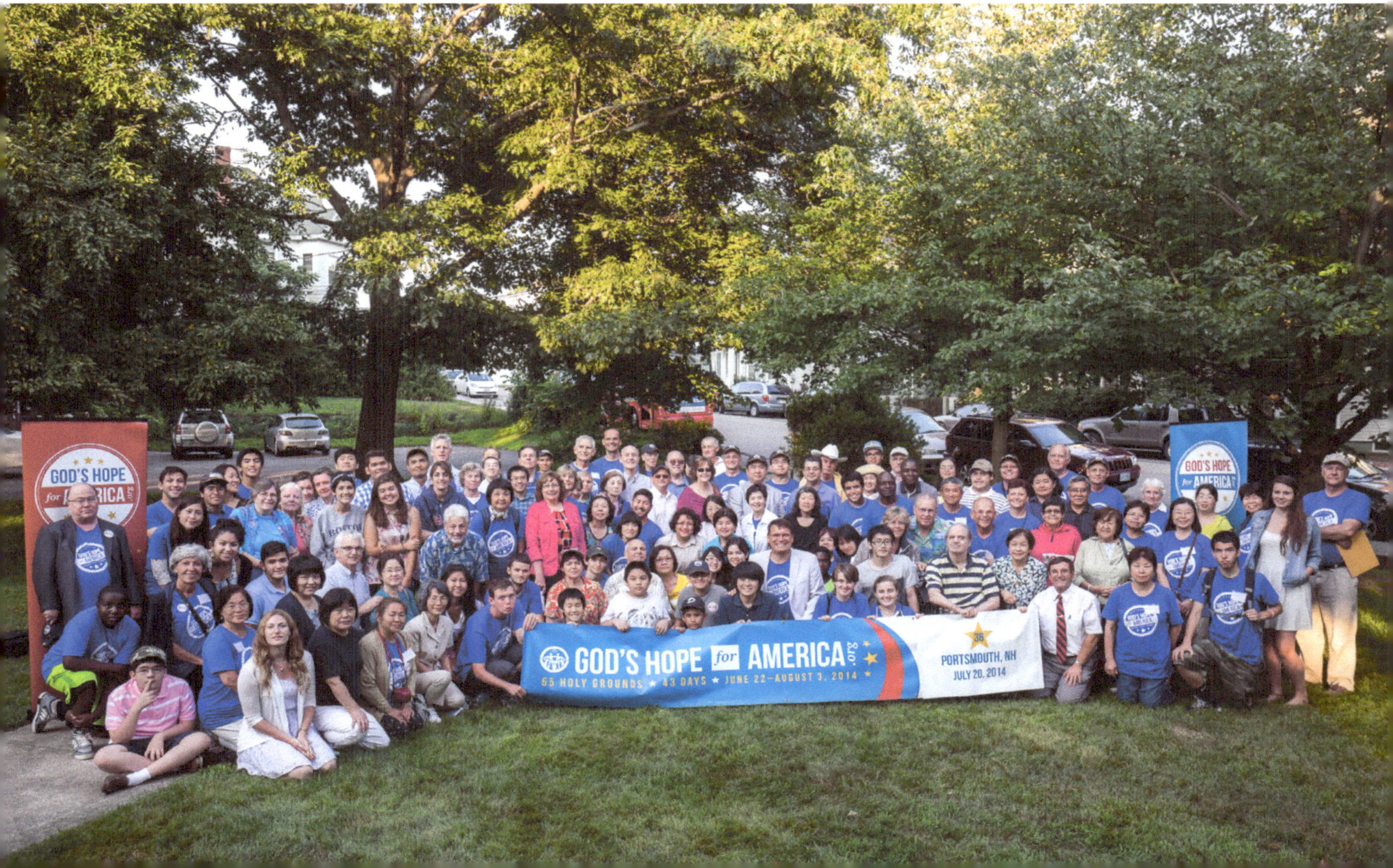
GOD'S HOPE for AMERICA
65 HOLY GROUNDS ★ 43 DAYS ★ JUNE 22–AUGUST 3, 2014
36
PORTSMOUTH, NH
JULY 20, 2014
GOD'S HOPE
GOD'S HOPE for AMERICA

KITTERY, MAINE

HOLY GROUND ⭐ 36

EST: MARCH 19, 1965
GPS COORDINATES: 43°05'07.8"N 70°45'00.8"W

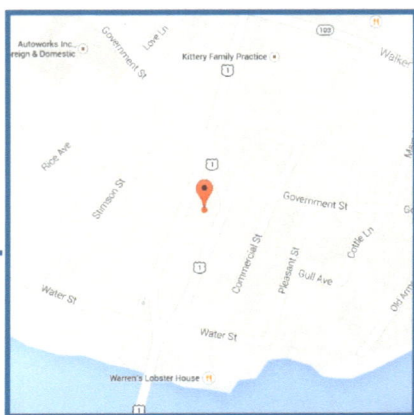

JOHN PAUL JONES HISTORIC SITE
13 Hunter Ave.,
Kittery, ME 03904

LOCATION

The Kittery Holy Ground is in a small city park named John Paul Jones Historic Site, located between two neighborhood streets. It is marked by an evergreen tree toward the north end of the park. You can park in the lot on the corner of Pleasant Street and Water Street and make your way down the hill to the Holy Ground. Rev. Moon said Maine is shaped like a handle. If Maine can come together under God, then it can scoop the whole country up and God can claim America

JOURNAL ENTRY

Although it was night, their day was not yet finished, for they still had to reach the state of Maine. The small town of Kittery, Maine, a half-hour drive from Portsmouth, received the greatest honor in its history as Rev. Moon blessed its city park. While peacefully sleeping, the quiet village of Kittery received the blessing for that northern state.

To Mrs. Moon

Please become the highest, most precious and victorious True Mother. I am also striving to become the True Father, who lives for the sake of heaven and earth. This is the only thing in my mind. Please take good care of yourself.

-Rev. Moon, March 20, 1965, Brattleboro, VT

GOD'S HOPE
for AMERICA
Remember • Revive • Reimagine

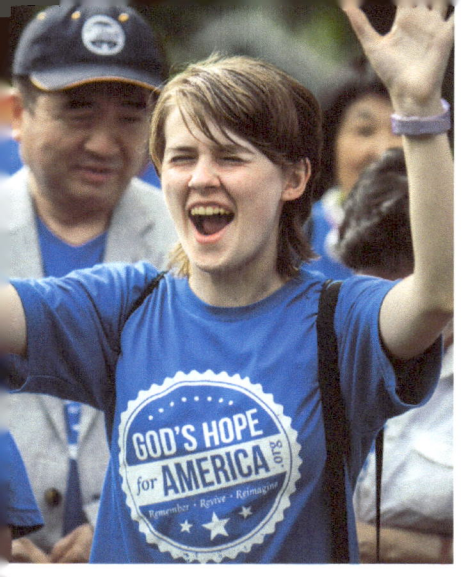

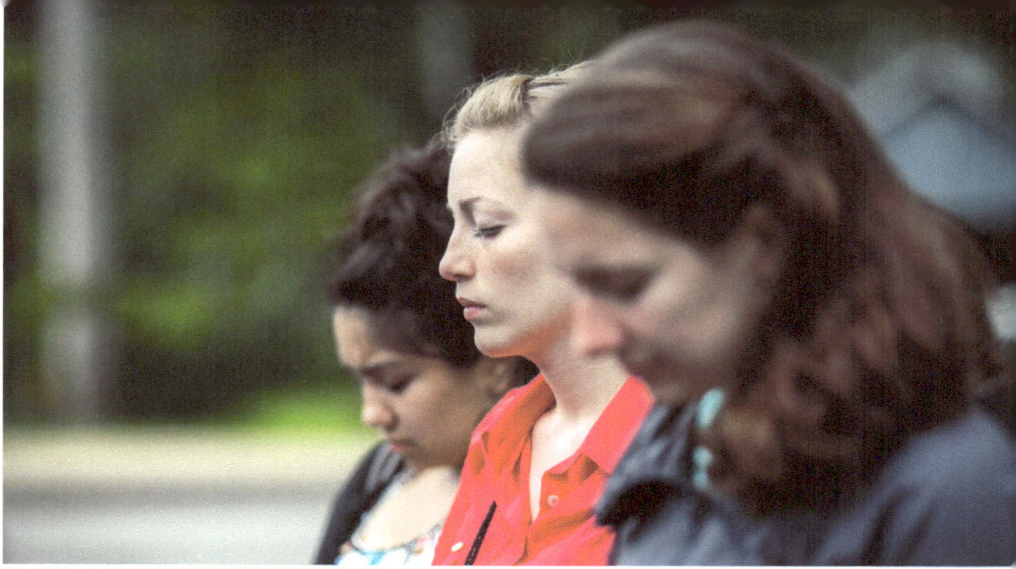

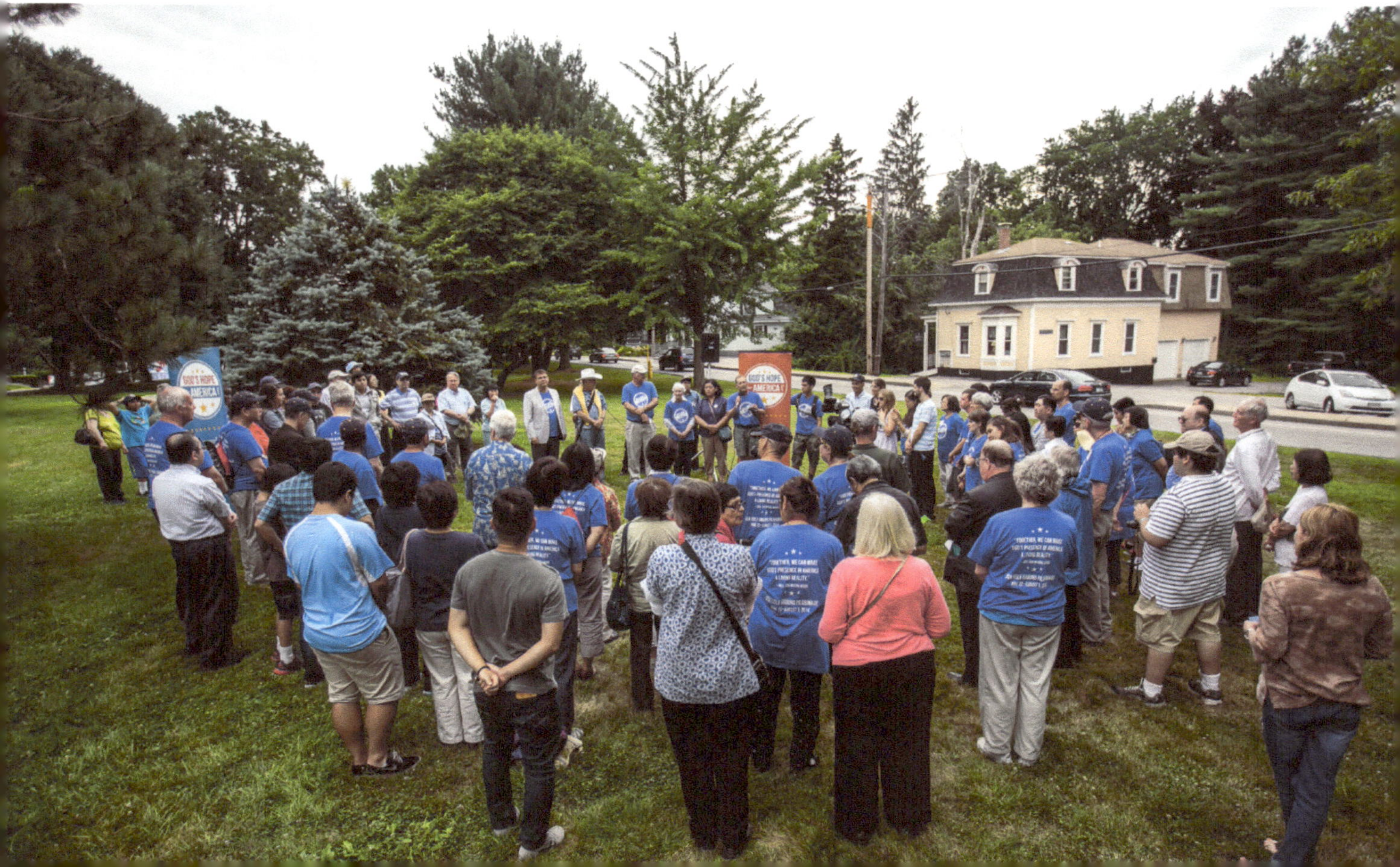
GOD'S HOPE
AMERICA

BRATTLEBORO, VERMONT

HOLY GROUND ⭐ 37

EST: MARCH 20, 1965
GPS COORDINATES: 42°51'27.4"N 72°33'35.7"W

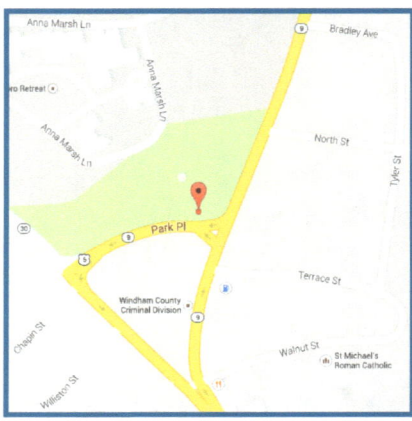

THE COMMON
Park Pl,
Brattleboro, VT 05301

LOCATION

The Brattleboro Holy Ground is located in a city park named The Common. It was originally marked by the middle tree in a row of three large trees bordering Putney Rd. on the northeast side of the park. The original tree is now gone; however, the imprint of where the tree once stood in the ground remains visible. There are two more new, tall trees surrounding the area.

JOURNAL ENTRY

Pressing onward through the chill and frosty night scene of New Hampshire and Vermont, they reached their destination: Brattleboro, Vermont, at 3 a.m. on March 20. They had a short rest, because as tired as they were, the sky had barely begun to lighten when Rev. Moon woke them up and urged them on. With haste, they found City Park and blessed its ground.

To Mrs. Moon

After a busy day, we stayed at the Holly Motel in Brattleboro, Vermont. And just before leaving there, I picked up my pen to write you. Today we are busy getting ready to depart for Cleveland, Ohio. I'm sorry that I only have a short time to write and convey news to you.

-Rev. Moon, March 20, 1965, Brattleboro, VT

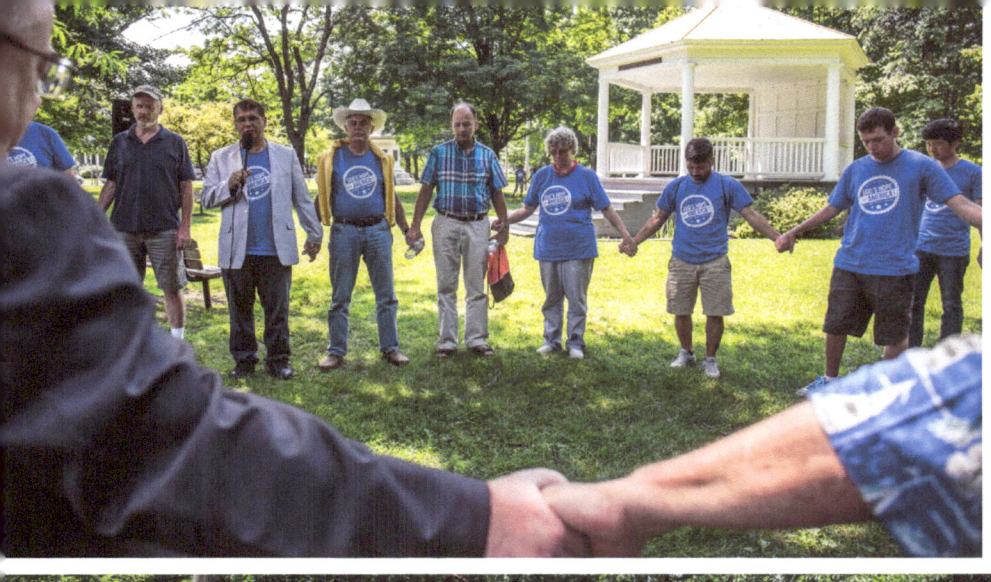

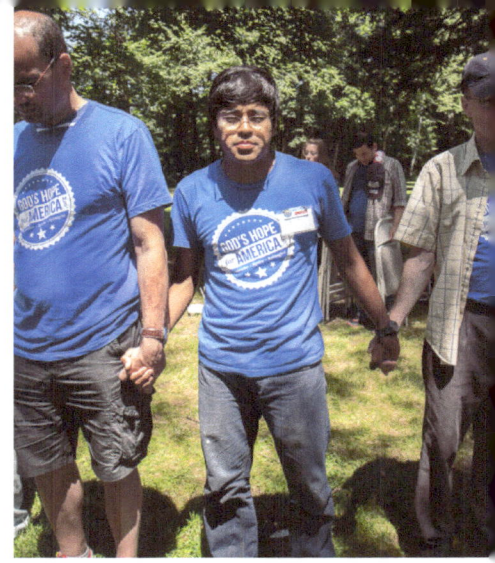

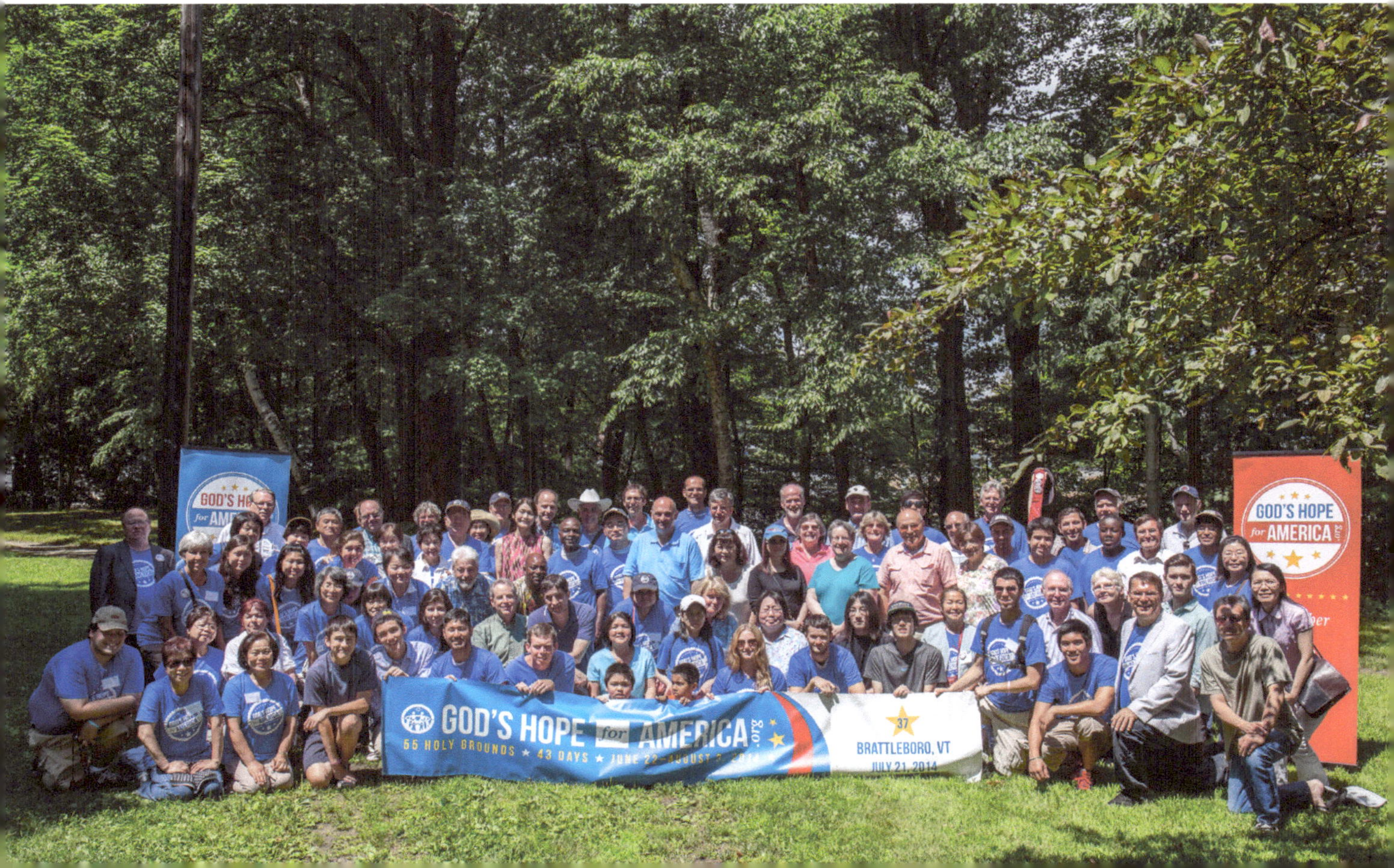
GOD'S HOPE for AMERICA .org
55 HOLY GROUNDS ★ 43 DAYS ★ JUNE 22–AUGUST 3,
37
BRATTLEBORO, VT
JULY 21, 2014
GOD'S HOPE for AMERICA .org

THE MIDWEST
FIELDS OF GRAIN

REGION E

TRAVEL TIME: MARCH 20, 1965 - MARCH 22, 1965

Embracing the northern edge of the country, the Midwest tour passes by Niagara Falls and the Great Lakes and ends just before the Mississippi River, a reminder of God's ever-flowing blessings.

"If America wants to keep the blessing of God as the leading nation of the world, it must form a partnership with God. Do you have God in your homes? Do you truly have God in your church? Do you have God in your society and nation? God is the cement."

—Rev. Moon, "God's Hope for America," Yankee Stadium, New York, June 1, 1976

E MIDWEST

CHECKLIST OF HOLY GROUNDS

- ☐ Cleveland, OH
- ☐ Detroit, MI
- ☐ Hammond, IN
- ☐ Chicago, IL
- ☐ Madison, WI

UNIFICATION THEOLOGICAL SEMINARY

EST: SEPTEMBER 20, 1975
GPS COORDINATES: 42°0'12.3"N 73°55'28.3"W

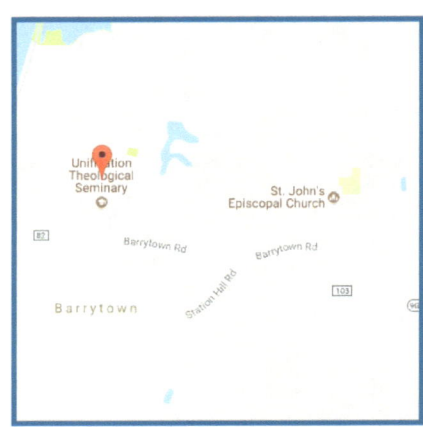

BARRYTOWN, NY
30 Seminary Dr.,
Barrytown, NY 12507

INTERFAITH EDUCATION

Another important part of the pilgrimage is visiting places important to the Moons. The Unification Theological Seminary in Barrytown, New York, a former Christian Brothers school and seminary about a hundred miles north of New York City, is one of those places. Rev. Moon spent more time here than at any of the Holy Grounds in the United States; he visited UTS over 100 times in the 1970s and 1980s.

Rev. Moon did not make a Holy Ground at UTS, but he made it holy by his personal investment of hours and days on end here in the early years of the Unification movement in America. He had a vision that the Christian leaders would be so impressed by UTS students that they would hire UTS graduates as clergy for their dying churches. God told Rev. Moon of this vision, "Do it here." The task is handed to the next generation to fulfill this vision.

DID YOU KNOW?

- Rev. Moon loved the students, who came from many different faith backgrounds. He loved to playfully challenge the faculty to think from new perspectives.

He loved communing with God and with nature. Most of all, he loved to fish. He created long nets to cover the entrances to South Bay from the Hudson River to catch the carp that swam there in abundance.

NIAGARA FALLS, NY

VISITED: MARCH 20, 1965
GPS COORDINATES: 43°5'12.2"N 79°3'59.4"W

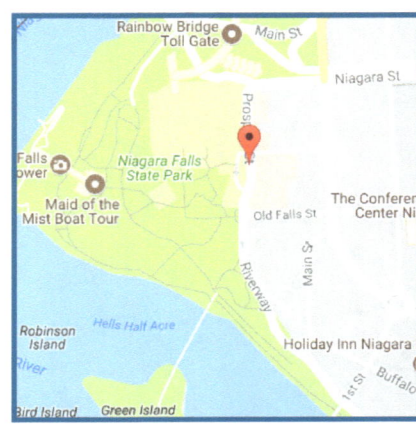

NIAGARA FALLS STATE PARK
332 Prospect St,
Niagara Falls, NY 14303

LOCATION

"I want my power and gusto to be even greater than Niagara Falls," said Rev. Moon when he arrived at the falls during his first tour of America. Since it was a stop Rev. Moon made on his original tour, the God's Hope for America Pilgrimage stopped as well and offered a prayer.

JOURNAL ENTRY

The next stop was Niagara Falls. It was a long drive across New York State, but they reached the Falls by late afternoon. The ground was covered with snow and the spray from the roaring falls froze onto their clothes as they stood by the water's edge. The sheer power of so much water plunging nonstop over the cliffs made them feel small, indeed; and once again they marveled at the magnificence of God's handiwork. Yet Rev. Moon had taught them that creation is only a reflection of their own image. One little person is much more important than the greatest and most awesome object of creation. They turned to go, feeling exhilarated—and very cold.

DID YOU KNOW?

- Rev. Moon walked on his original trip, from Goat Island to the American Falls and then over the Rainbow Bridge to view the Horshoe Falls from the Canadian side.

CLEVELAND, OHIO

HOLY GROUND ⭐ 38

EST: MARCH 20, 1965
GPS COORDINATES: 41°30'26.1"N 81°36'40.9"W

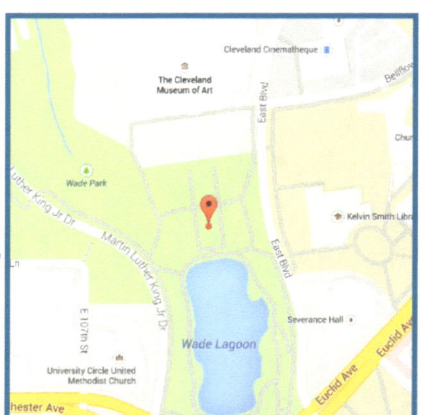

WADE PARK
11175 East Blvd.,
Cleveland, OH 44106

LOCATION

The Cleveland Holy Ground is located in Wade Park in the University Circle neighborhood. It is in the exact center of the lawn between the lagoon and the museum.

JOURNAL ENTRY

Leaving Niagara Falls and Buffalo behind, they plunged into a raging Lake Erie blizzard which lasted the 200 miles to Cleveland, Ohio. They had to slow down, as the driver squinted into the swirling whiteness and kept a tight grip on the wheel. Not many cars were on the road now. Occasionally, snow plows whizzed by in pairs, looming out of the blizzard like friendly monsters. They were glad to see the smiling faces of the Cleveland members and sit down to steaming dishes of rice and meat!

To Mrs. Moon

Despite the busy days traveling through the northern part of America. I still want to stay in touch with you, so I am writing. Unlike the southern states, the northern states are cold this time of year. The weather is changing, but there are still many snowy days when we must drive very carefully.

-Rev. Moon, March 25, 1965, Denver, CO

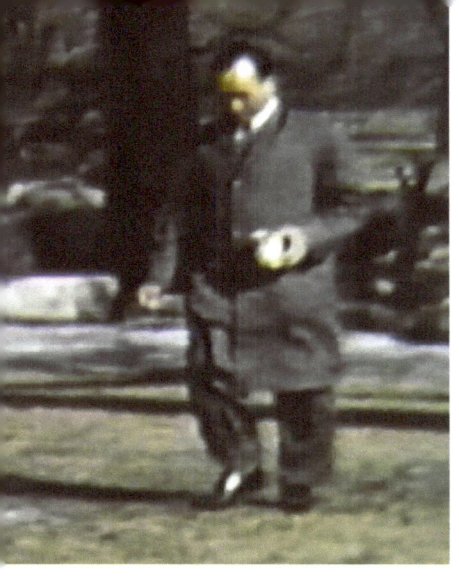

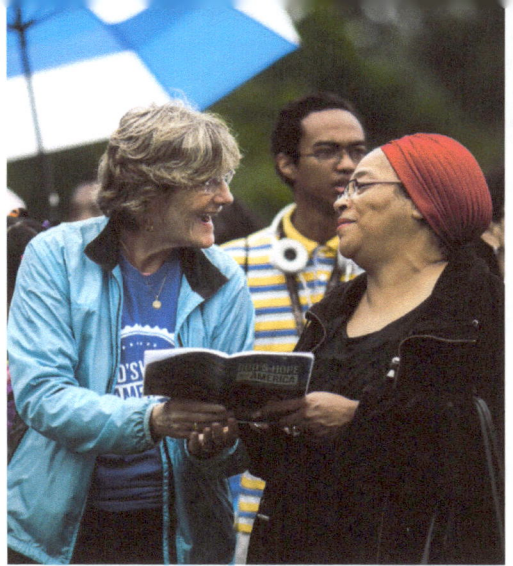

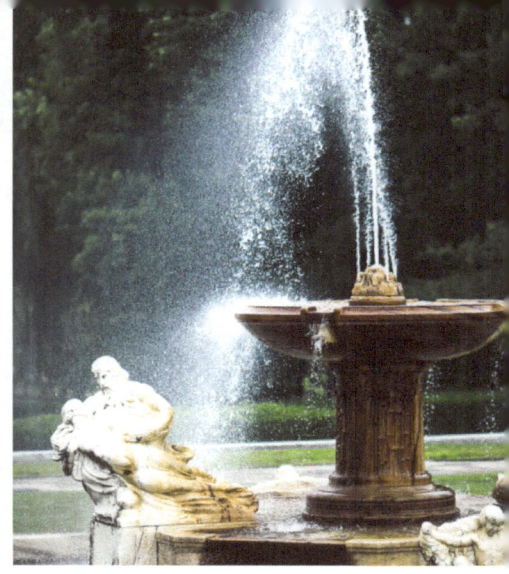

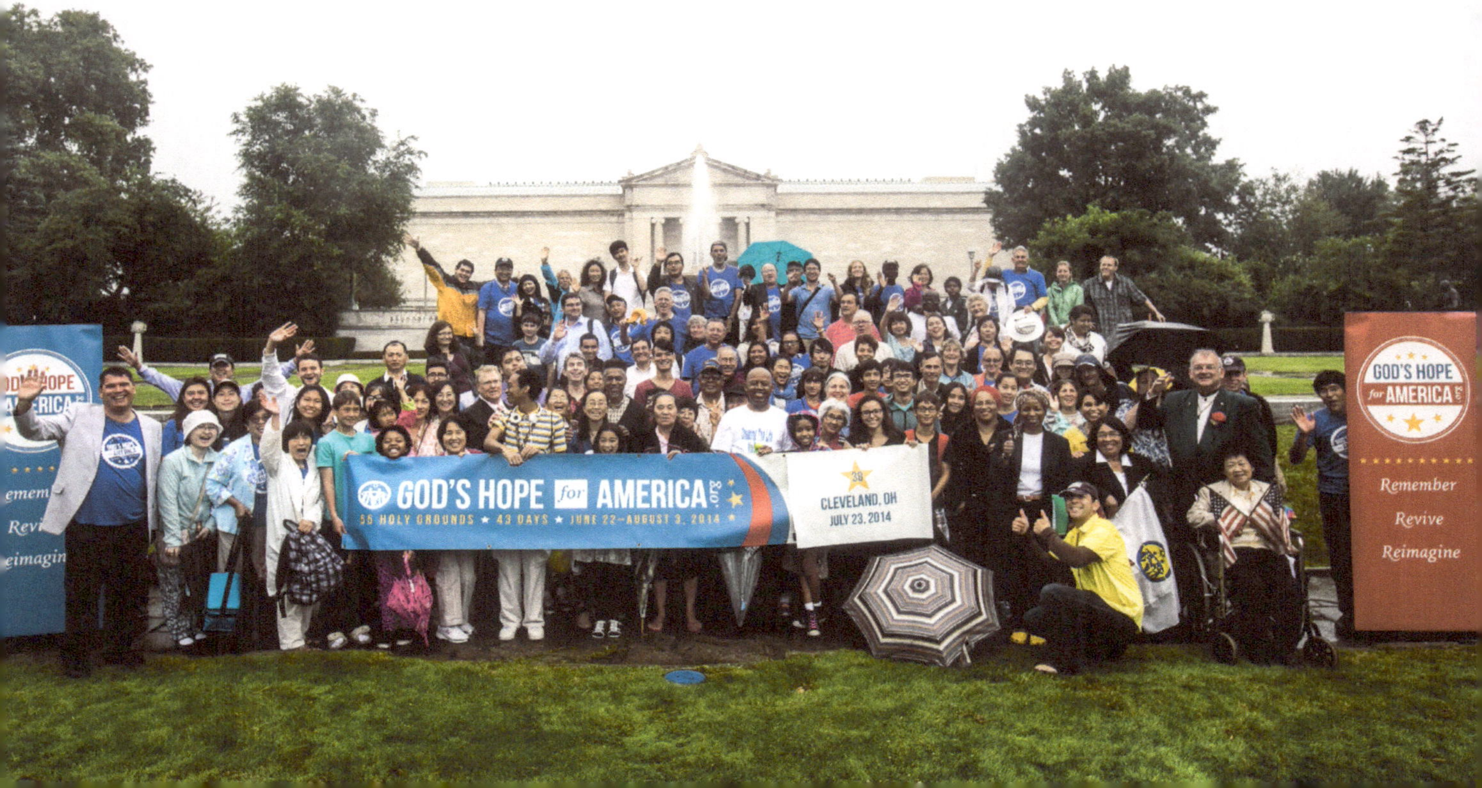
GOD'S HOPE for AMERICA
55 HOLY GROUNDS ★ 43 DAYS ★ JUNE 22—AUGUST 3, 2014
38
CLEVELAND, OH
JULY 23, 2014
GOD'S HOPE for AMERICA
Remember
Revive
Reimagine

DETROIT, MICHIGAN

HOLY GROUND ⭐ 39

EST: MARCH 21, 1965
GPS COORDINATES: 42°20'21.5"N 82°59'03.7"W

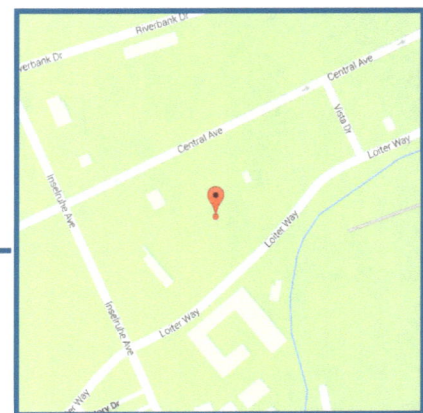

BELLE ISLE PARK
15 Loiter Way,
Detroit, MI 48207

LOCATION

The Detroit Holy Ground is in Belle Isle Park, an island and vast park located right between the city of Detroit and Canada. In a field across from a large Tudor-styled brick building on Loiter Way near Inselruhe St., the Holy Ground is marked by a large stone with a plaque.

JOURNAL ENTRY

After a comfortable night's rest and a hearty breakfast, they left on March 21 for Detroit, Michigan, the next city to receive Rev. Moon's blessing.

DID YOU KNOW?

- Dr. Martin Luther King Jr. was in Detroit the day before Rev. Moon came to establish the Holy Ground in 1965. Imagine if they had met! Imagine if their paths had crossed, how they could have worked together. …

Holy Ground
Consecrated
March 21, 1965
By
Rev. & Mrs. Sun Myung Moon
on the first world tour
True love is to give and give and give
to forget that you have given,
and give again.

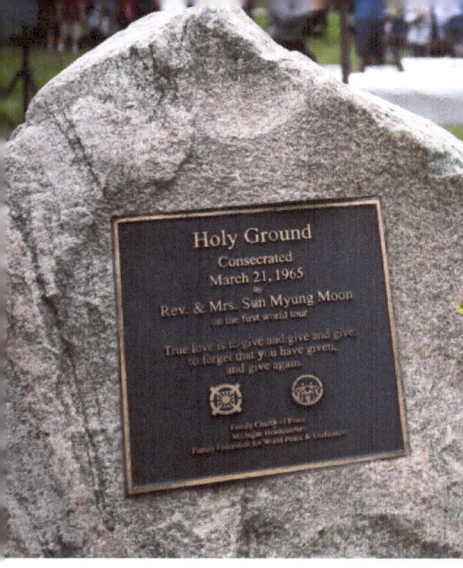

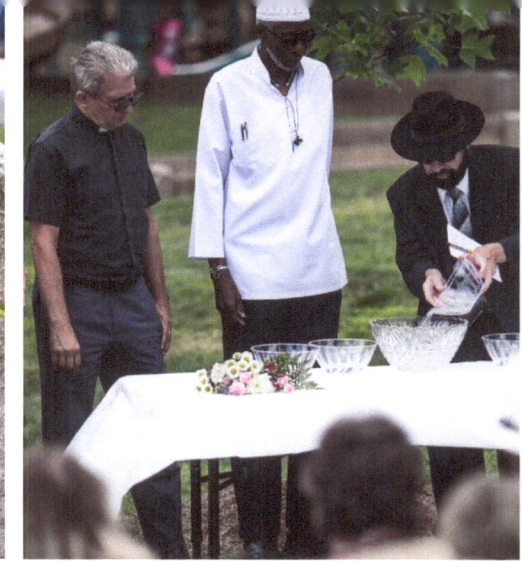

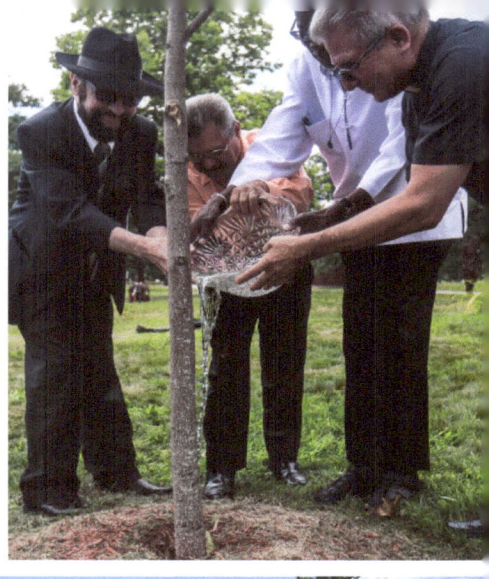

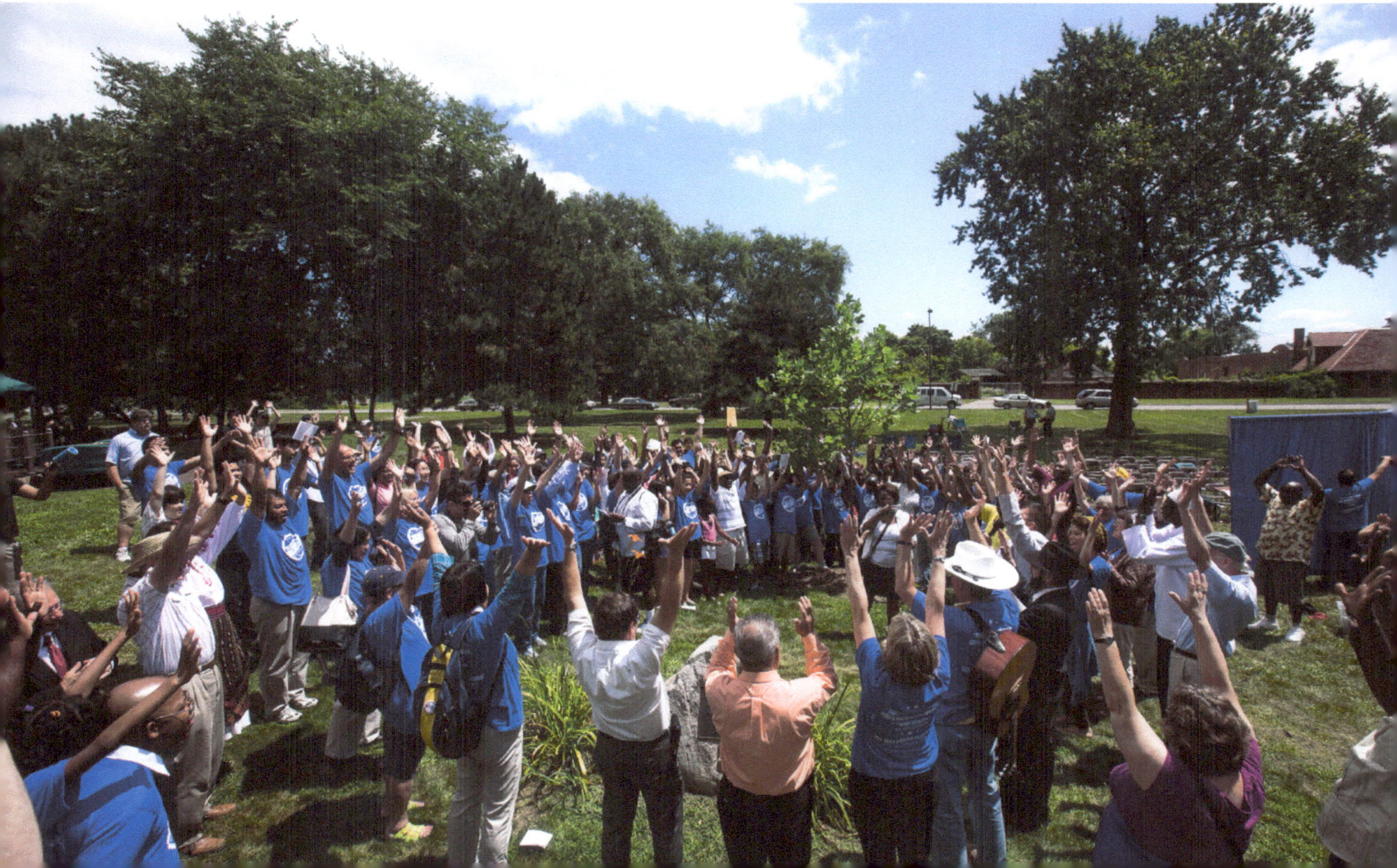

HAMMOND, INDIANA

HOLY GROUND

EST: MARCH 21, 1965
GPS COORDINATES: 41°36'27.3"N 87°31'16.4"W

HARRISON PARK
5781-5829 Hohman Ave.,
Hammond, IN 46320

LOCATION

The Hammond Holy Ground is located in Harrison Park. It was initially marked by a large tree near a lamp, west of a grocery store and east of a set of three small trees. However, the grocery store is now gone and the exact location of the Holy Ground tree is unknown.

JOURNAL ENTRY

They journeyed on across the snow-covered ground of Michigan and entered Indiana, where Rev. Moon blessed a park in the city of Hammond near Chicago.

To Mrs. Moon

Although I think about the great significance of traveling to these far places, still I often think how the course of restoration has been filled with sadness. ... I realize the vastness of this land and magnitude of heaven's providence. It makes me reflect on the labor required for heaven's providence of restoration.

-Rev. Moon, March 25, 1965, Denver, CO

CHICAGO, ILLINOIS

HOLY GROUND 41

EST: MARCH 21, 1965
GPS COORDINATES: 41°52'24.6"N 87°37'04.8"W

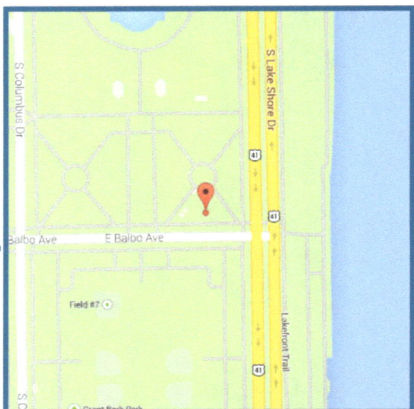

GRANT PARK
301 S. Columbus Dr.,
Chicago, IL 60605

LOCATION

The Chicago Holy Ground is located in downtown Chicago's Grant Park. It can be found in a group of trees near the corner of S. Columbus Dr. and E. Balbo Ave. The original trees were removed but the Holy Ground is now marked by new trees planted in their place.

JOURNAL ENTRY

Since Rev. Moon's purpose in coming to the United States was primarily to bless Holy Grounds, they were unable to stay in Chicago, or many other church centers, longer than one night, and after the ceremony the following morning they sadly said goodbye and set off for Madison, Wisconsin.

To Mrs. Moon

I am grateful that you have become a great example for many people. Only I know that great mission that you are trying to surmount and the cross of the heart that you carry. All I can do is pray that you will become the True Mother who will be exalted and honored by multitudes of people.

-Rev. Moon, March 25, 1965, Denver, CO

GOD'S HOPE for AMERICA
55 HOLY GROUNDS ★ 43 DAYS ★ JUNE 22–AUGUST 3, 2014
CHICAGO, IL
JULY 26, 2014

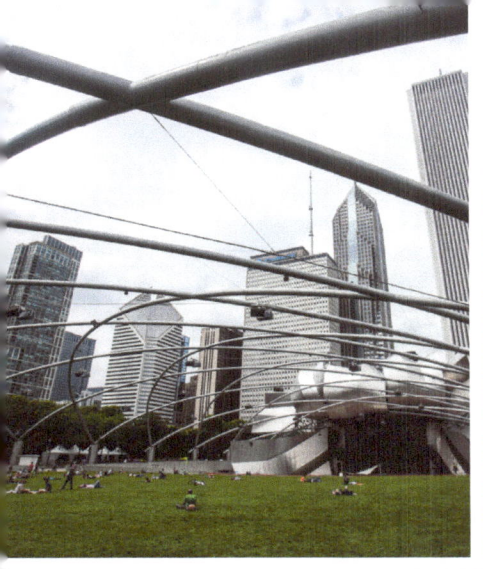

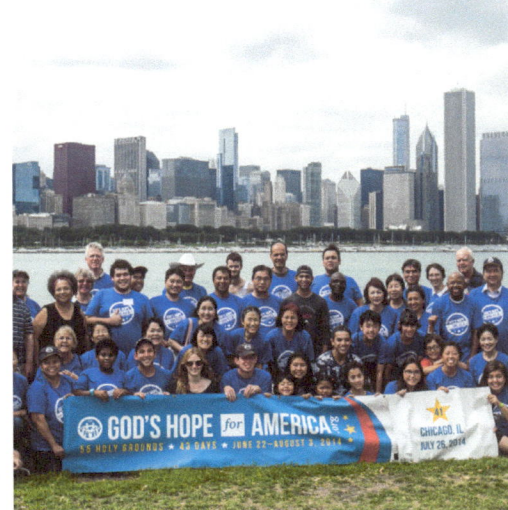

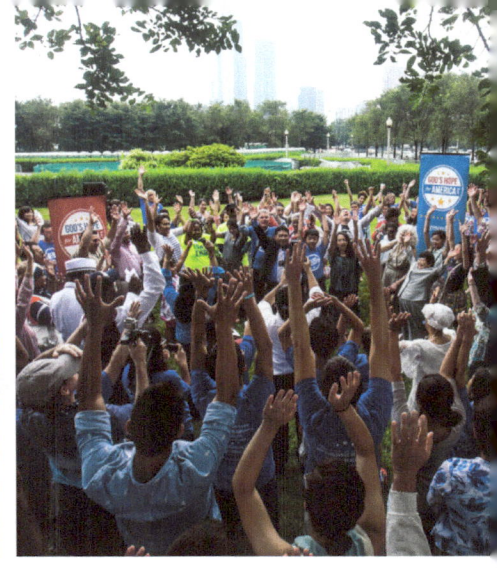

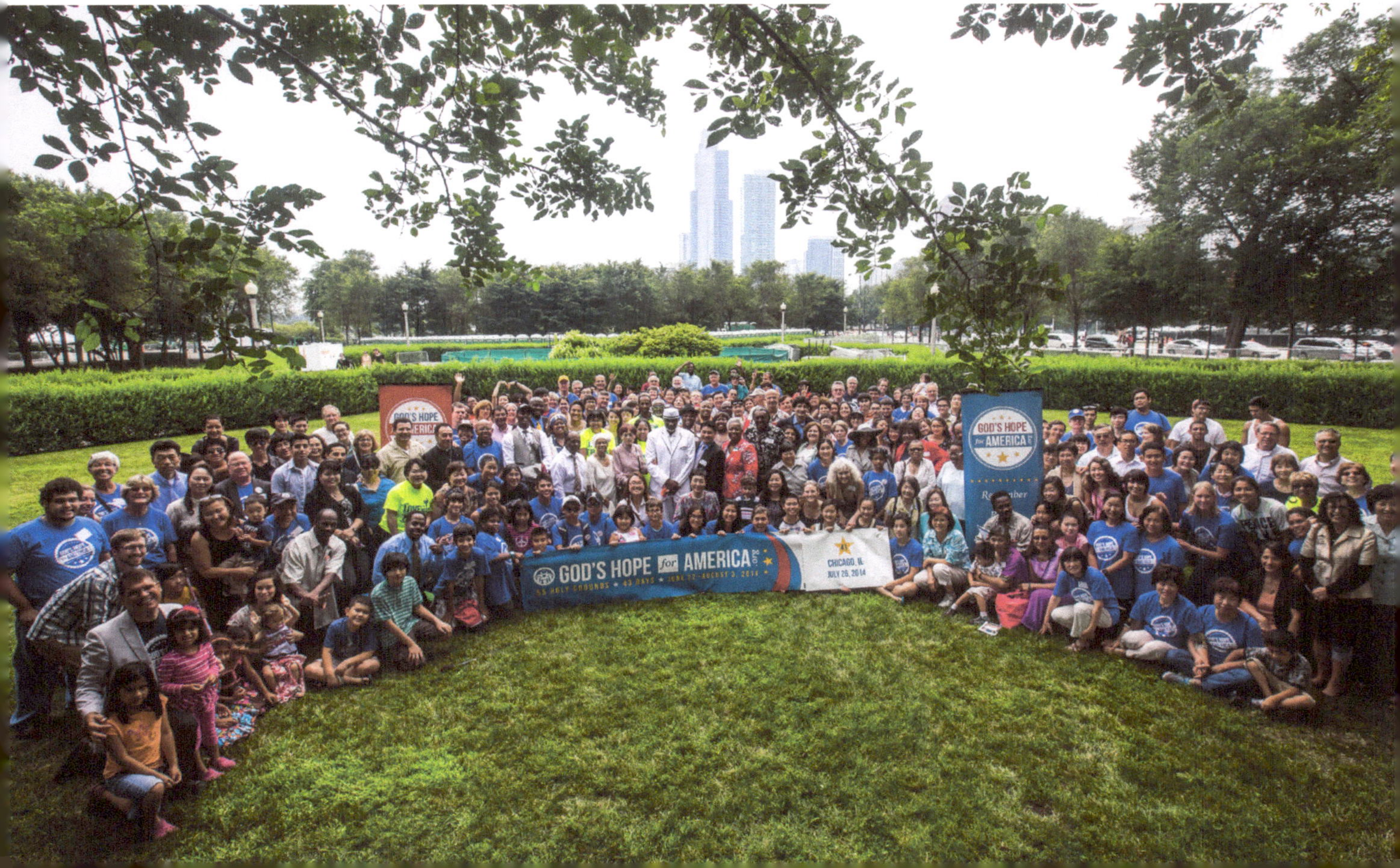
GOD'S HOPE for AMERICA
CHICAGO, IL
JULY 26, 2014

MADISON, WISCONSIN

HOLY GROUND 42

EST: MARCH 22, 1965
GPS COORDINATES: 43°04'08.9"N 89°26'28.4"W

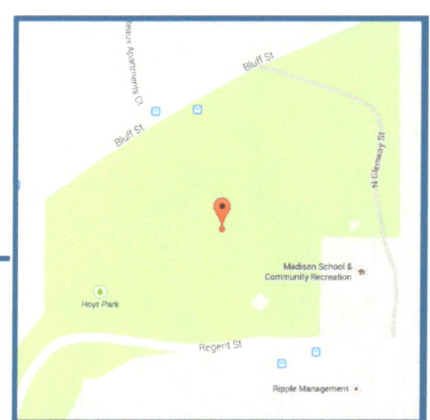

HOYT PARK
3802 Regent St.,
Madison, WI 53705

LOCATION

The Madison Holy Ground is located in Hoyt Park on Regent St., next to Hoyt School. It is marked by a large, freestanding oak tree standing alone north of a stone shelter house on the far side of a wide grassy field.

JOURNAL ENTRY

In Madison, they sat and talked with Mrs. Marjorie Hill, who had just completed the Divine Principle Correspondence Course lessons, and who had learned of their early arrival two days earlier. After having blessed a small park near her home, Rev. Moon and his party left Mrs. Hill, full of joy and somewhat dazzled by the swiftness of all that had transpired, and set off for the twin cities of Minneapolis and St. Paul, Minnesota, separated by the Mississippi River.

HELPFUL TIPS

- This Holy Ground is as far back in the park as you can get. Walk past the stone pavilion, the basketball courts, the playground, through the field and right up to the woods where the big oak stands.

"TOGETHER, WE CAN MAKE
GOD'S PRESENCE IN AMERICA
A LIVING REALITY."

GOD'S HOPE
AMERICA

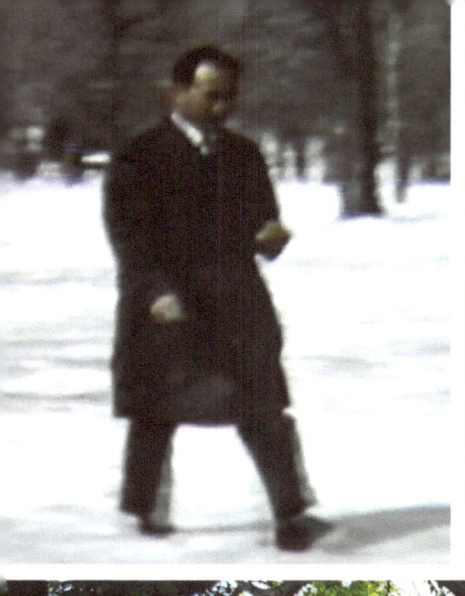

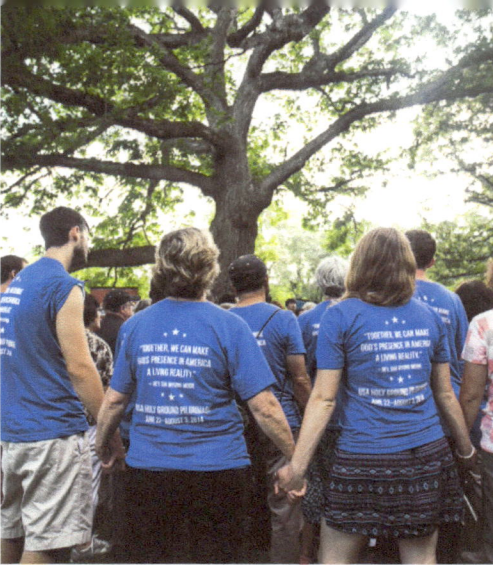

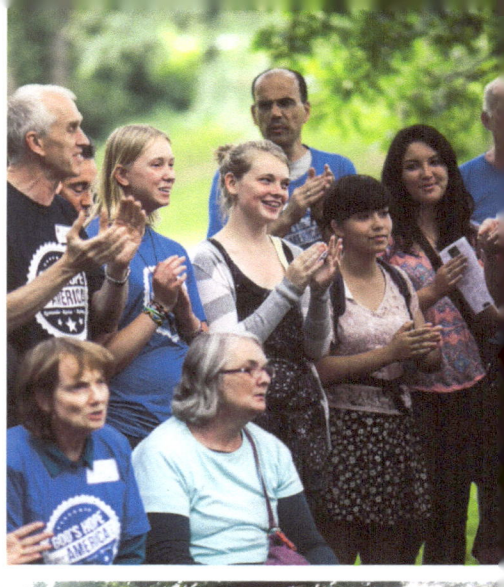

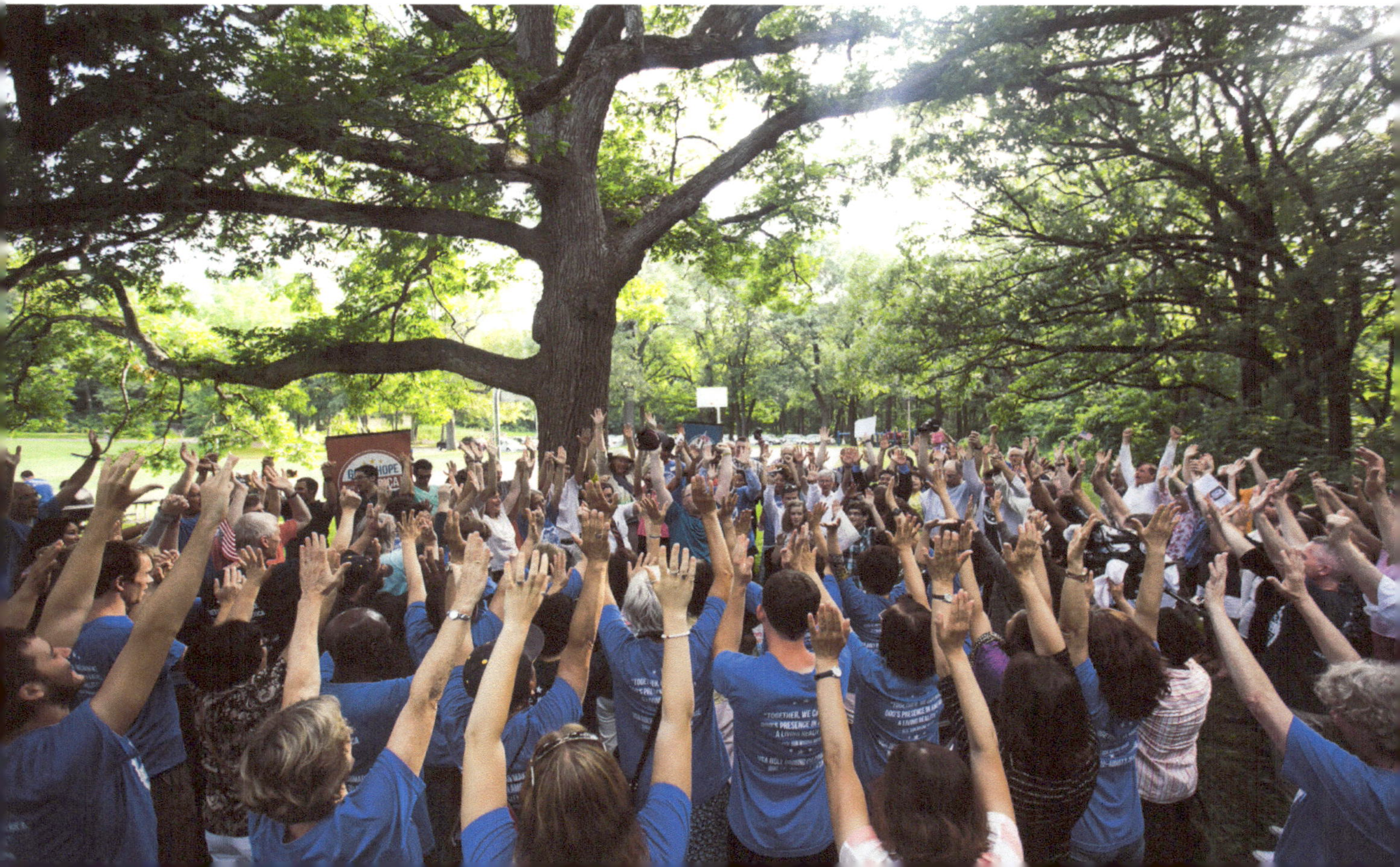

PURPLE MOUNTAIN MAJESTY

REGION F

TRAVEL TIME: MARCH 23, 1965 - MARCH 29, 1965

F MOUNTAINS

Driving through the Western landscape, the Dakotas and the Rocky Mountains is a journey of pure awe. The cascading waterfalls and fortress of mountains instill a sense of surrender before God.

"Put yourself in the position of total reliance on God. What a wonderful faith! This touches the heart of God. And when God is moved, He offers promises; and when He makes promises, He will fulfill them."

–Rev. Moon, "God's Hope for America," Washington, D.C. October 21, 1973

CHECKLIST OF HOLY GROUNDS

- ☐ St. Paul, MN
- ☐ Fargo, ND
- ☐ Sioux Falls, SD
- ☐ Sioux City, IA
- ☐ Lincoln, NE
- ☐ Cheyenne, WY
- ☐ Denver, CO
- ☐ Salt Lake City, UT
- ☐ Boise, ID
- ☐ Missoula, MT
- ☐ Seattle, WA
- ☐ Eugene, OR

ST. PAUL, MINNESOTA

HOLY GROUND

EST: MARCH 23, 1965
GPS COORDINATES: 44°58'57.4"N 93°08'40.6"W

LOCATION

The St. Paul Holy Ground is located in Como Regional Park. It sits on the highest hill above the Como Lakeside Pavilion and Black Bear Crossings. Although the original tree has been removed, the Holy Ground area remains. Visit the nearby Korean War Memorial, honoring the 750,000 veterans from Minnesota who passed away during the Korean War.

JOURNAL ENTRY

Rev. Moon smiled when they arrived in St. Paul, Minnesota. He liked the idea of staying in a city named after Paul of Jesus' time. He loves Paul and feels close to him in many ways as St. Paul accomplished so much to lay a foundation for Christianity. When they walked to the Holy Ground site the snow reached halfway up their legs, and they were only too glad to follow in Rev. Moon's footsteps. At every point of the journey, his energy abounded, his zeal was unflagging, and his pace was untiring.

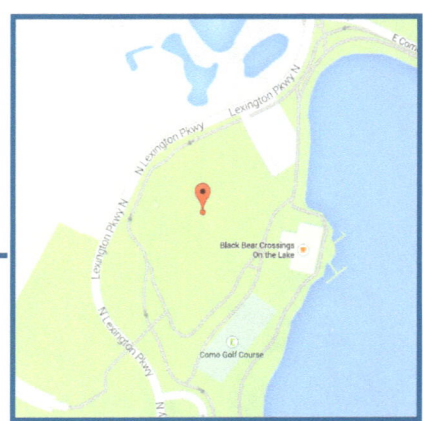

COMO REGIONAL PARK
1360 Lexington Pkwy. N.,
St. Paul, MN 55103

To Mrs. Moon

I am so grateful that you pray for me and accompany me in heart wherever I go. I also salute you for taking such an important responsibility. ... I hope that one day you and I will be able to travel around America together.

-Rev. Moon, March 25, 1965, Denver, CO

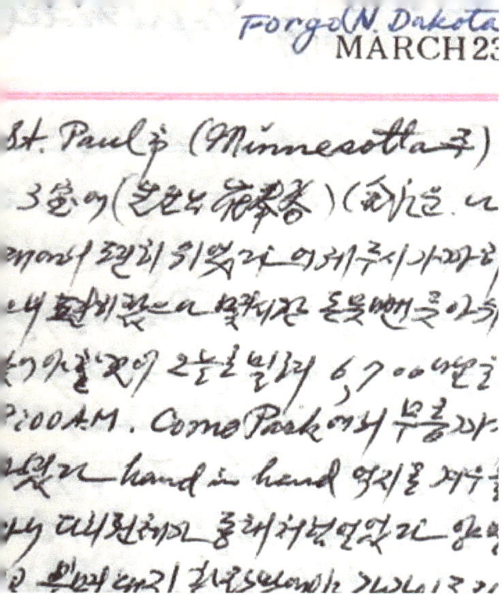

Fargo (N. Dakota)
MARCH 23

St. Paul은 (Minnesotta주)
3월에 (몬타나 洲總會) (하기는. 나
에게서 떨치 되었다. 의게주시 가까도
내 형제같은 성책이전 돗꼭빼준 아송
가있갈것이 오늘로 밀려 6,700여명들
9:00 A.M. Como Park에서 무릎과
와었고 hand in hand 영리를 저우슬
며 대천해고 풀해처님없던가. 있을
을 본며 대지 찬드섯이에 가보디그 ?

FARGO, N. DAKOTA

HOLY GROUND 44

EST: MARCH 23, 1965
GPS COORDINATES: 46°52'14.1"N 96°47'12.6"W

LOCATION

The Fargo Holy Ground is located in Island Park atop a hill dotted with pine trees. It is east of the park's playground, marked by a tree with double trunks. It might be easiest to find the Holy Ground by parking on 4th Street in front of The Stage at Island Park theater, then climbing up the hill to the left of the theatre. The Holy Ground is among the first couple of trees in the row.

JOURNAL ENTRY

After Minnesota, they drove on into the vast frozen North. In Fargo, North Dakota, there wasn't as much snow on the ground and the sun was shining, but the temperature was 16 below zero—and that was at noon! They rubbed their hands together vigorously and stamped their feet to keep warm—but not Rev. Moon. He didn't even wear his gloves. He concentrated fully on the ceremony and didn't seem to notice that his fingers had quickly become red and stiff.

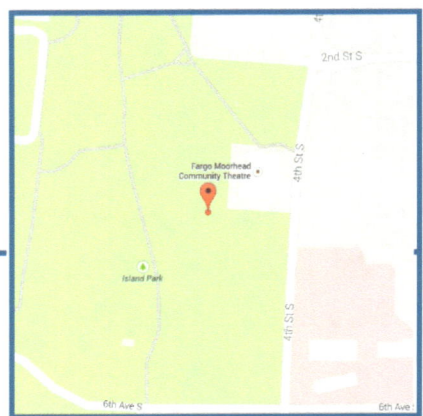

ISLAND PARK
302 7th St. S.,
Fargo, ND 58103

To Mrs. Moon

I think you must be going through many experiences during your busy life in Seoul. I am so sorry that you are unable to live an easygoing life. My heart goes out to you, knowing that you must always be careful in your public life, lived among numerous people who are centered on the Will.

-Rev. Moon, March 25, 1965, Denver, CO

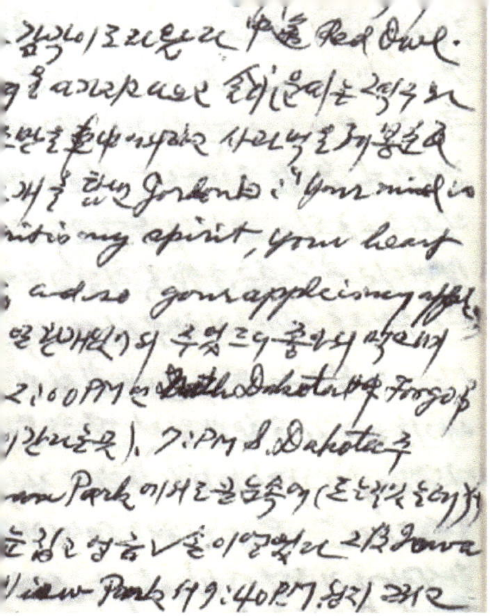
Red Owl
your mind is
my spirit, your heart
7:PM S. Dakota
Park
9:40 PM

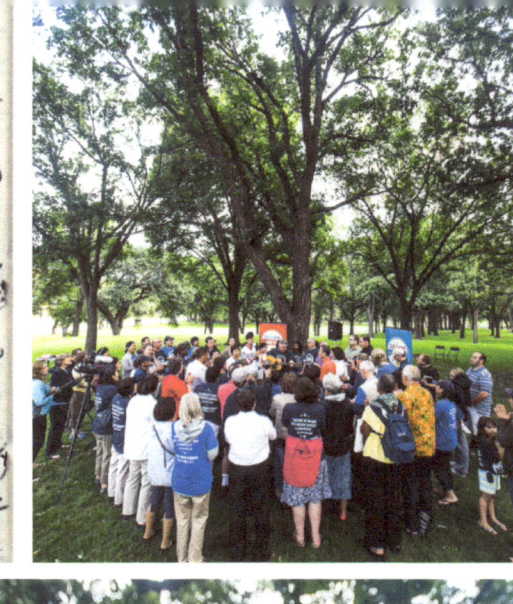

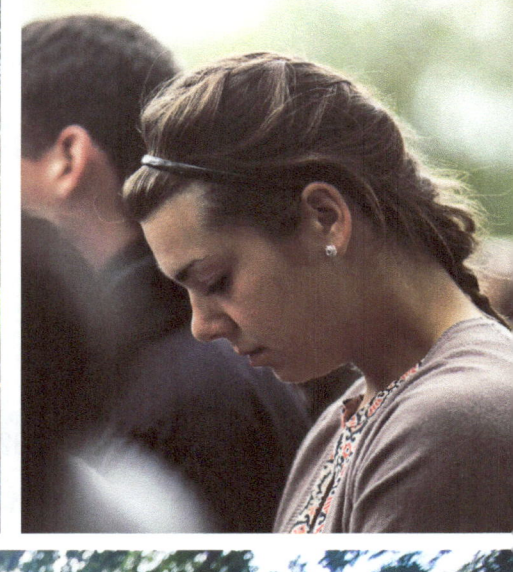

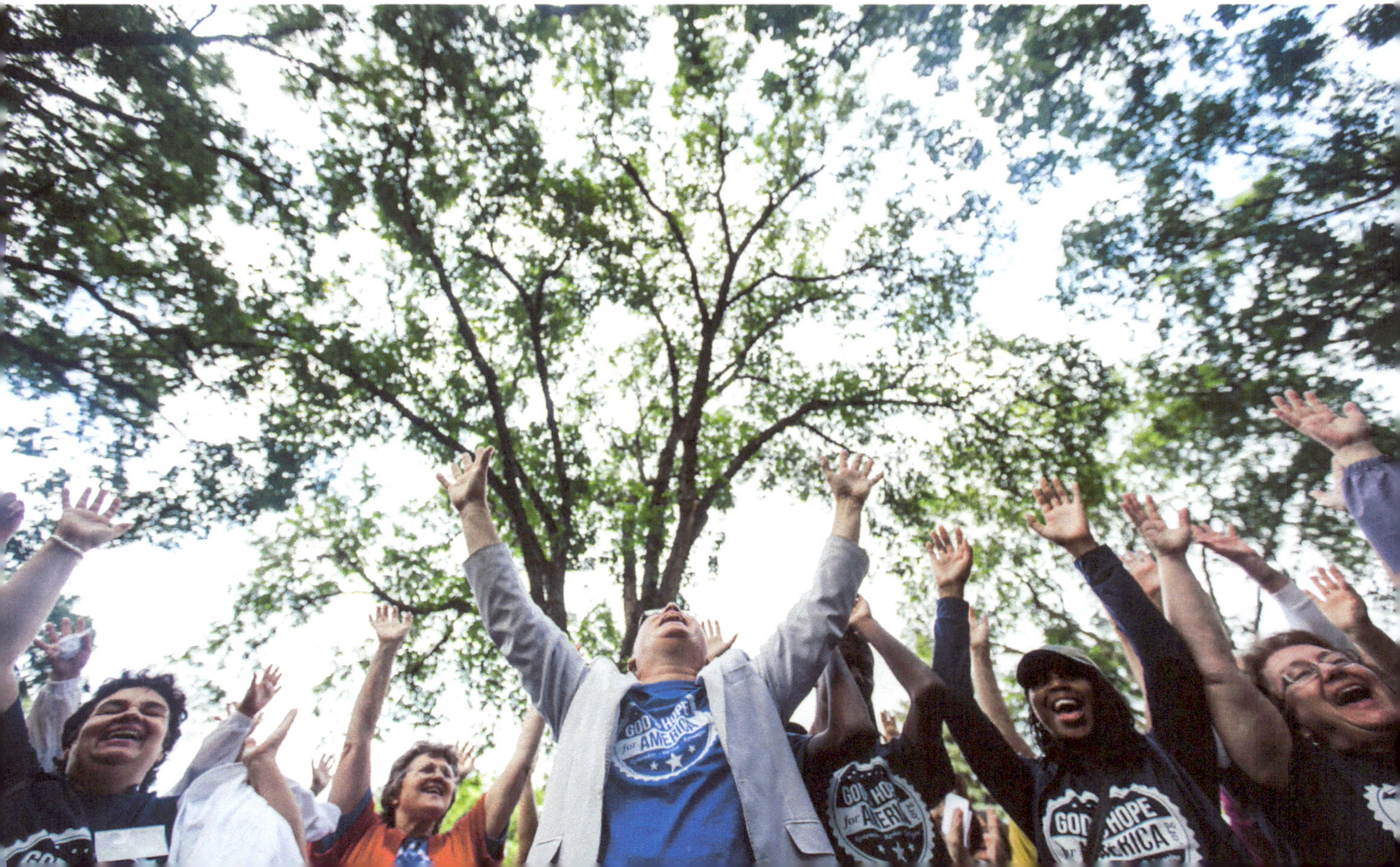

SIOUX FALLS,
S. DAKOTA

HOLY GROUND 45

EST: MARCH 23, 1965
GPS COORDINATES: 43°32'06.8"N 96°45'47.6"W

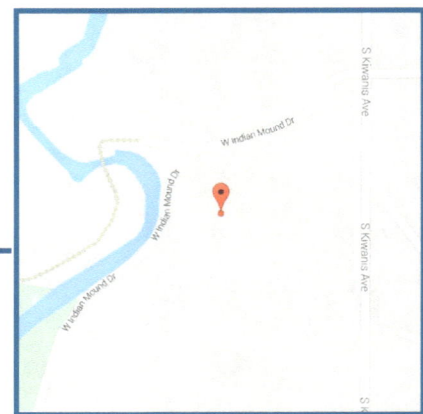

SHERMAN PARK
22nd and Kiwanis,
Sioux Falls, SD 57103

LOCATION

The Sioux Falls Holy Ground is located in Sherman Park atop a hill, at the site of a 1,600-year old Native American burial ground. It is near five historic Indian burial mounds and is marked by a tree on top of a high hill.

JOURNAL ENTRY

Surprisingly enough, South Dakota offered little hindrance in the form of snow or ice, and the group made good time through the flat expanse of the state, reaching Sioux Falls by early evening. Like most of the blessings in cold weather, the ceremony at the summit was brief.

WHILE IN THE AREA

- Take a moment to read the historical information posted on signs at the Holy Ground site. They provide fascinating insight into the Native American history of the area.

- Near the Holy Ground site is Sioux Falls, with its layers of golden rock and rushing waters, as well as a cafe and historical ruins.

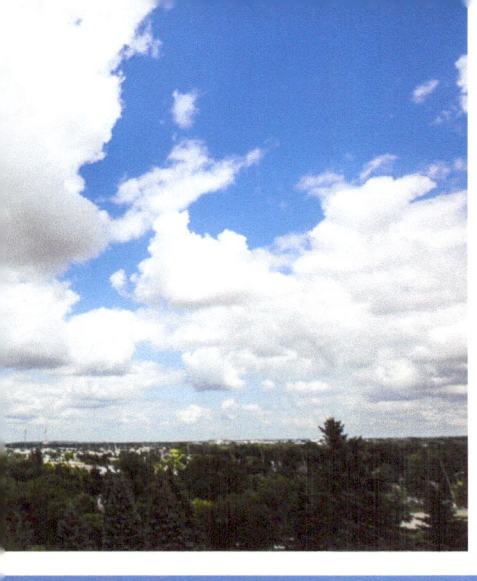

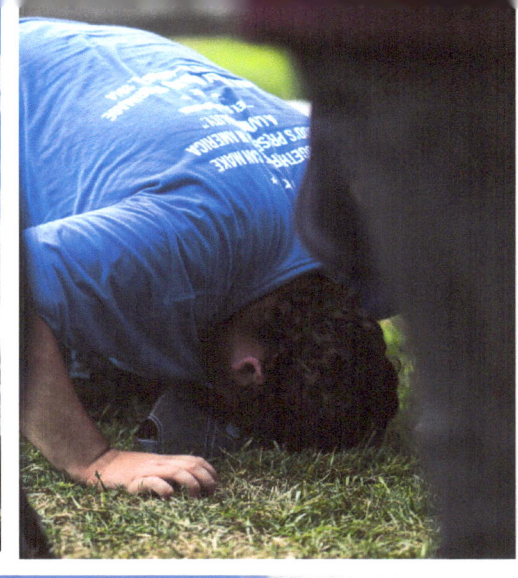

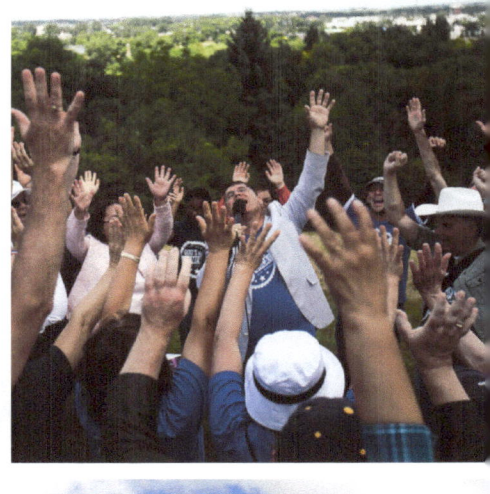

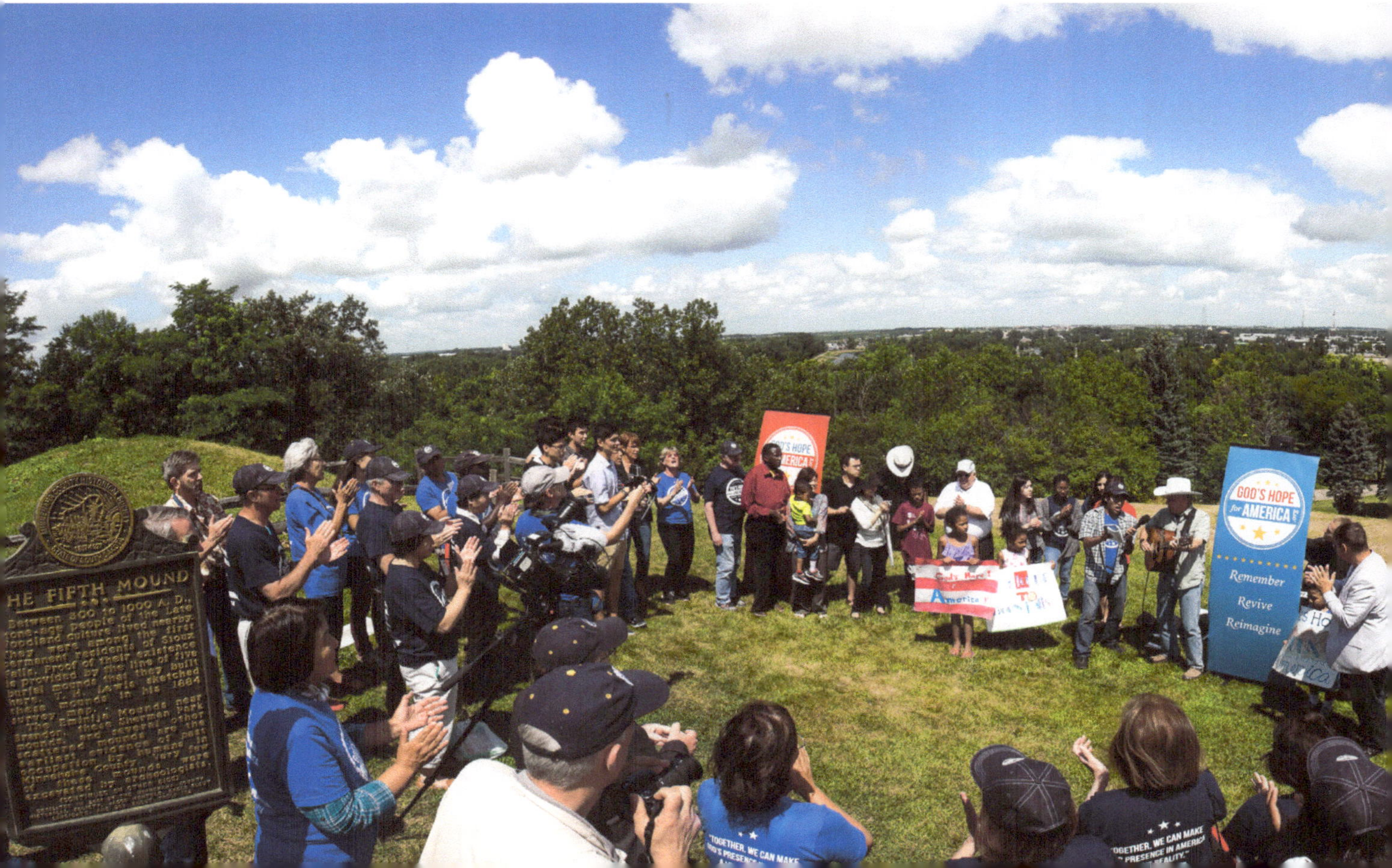
HE FIFTH MOUND
GOD'S HOPE for AMERICA
Remember
Revive
Reimagine

SIOUX CITY, IOWA

HOLY GROUND ⭐ 46

EST: MARCH 23, 1965
GPS COORDINATES: 42°31'04.4"N 96°24'32.8"W

GRANDVIEW PARK
24th and Grandview,
Sioux City, IA 51104

LOCATION

The Sioux City Holy Ground is located in Grandview Park, near the 24th St. entrance. Originally a lamppost marked the location but the area has since become a parking lot. The Holy Ground location is still accessible near two water towers. Getting to the Holy Ground will mean driving up a winding hill through neighborhoods. Just remember that True Father always tried to pick the highest spot to make a Holy Ground, and that should help you find it!

JOURNAL ENTRY

In Sioux City, Iowa, there was another brief Holy Ground blessing.

To Mrs. Moon

Please give everyone my regards. Please explain to them that I cannot send letters to each of them. I assume that you are often anxious about the children. I try to picture them and imagine how they are growing up so quickly. Please always take care of your health and work diligently to pave the way.

-Rev. Moon, March 25, 1965, Denver, CO

LINCOLN, NEBRASKA

HOLY GROUND 47

EST: MARCH 24, 1965
GPS COORDINATES: 41°15'48.6"N 96°00'08.3"W

LOCATION

The Lincoln Holy Ground was originally located in Antelope Park. However this park was converted to the Lincoln Children's Zoo, and the Holy Ground is now believed to be a large, old tree inside the zoo's monkey enclosure. The new Holy Ground is located in Memorial Park, Omaha, at the peak of the park, across the street from the entrance to the war memorial.

JOURNAL ENTRY

Then to the overnight stop of Lincoln, Nebraska, at which another snowstorm enshrouded them with falling flakes. The hotel manager was very considerate and let them have three rooms for only $12.50. When they awoke the next morning, the world was a dazzling wonderland of white, and they had to sweep at least a foot of new snow off the car. They went to the site of the Holy Ground. Nearby was a small zoo where a flock of sheep watched silently as their True Shepherd sanctified the earth around them.

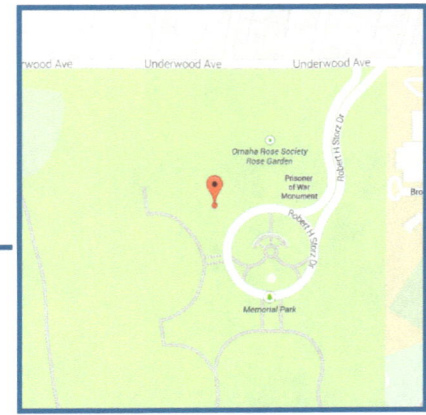

MEMORIAL PARK
6005 Underwood Ave., Omaha, NE 68132

To Mrs. Moon

When can I ever have enough time in my busy life for you? Once our youth is gone, it will never return, so let us cherish it and use each moment for the Will. I am sorry to bring this up every time I write you. ... the reason is, as a husband I have responsibility for you. ... anyway, who else can say such a thing to you?

-Rev. Moon, March 25, 1965, Denver, CO

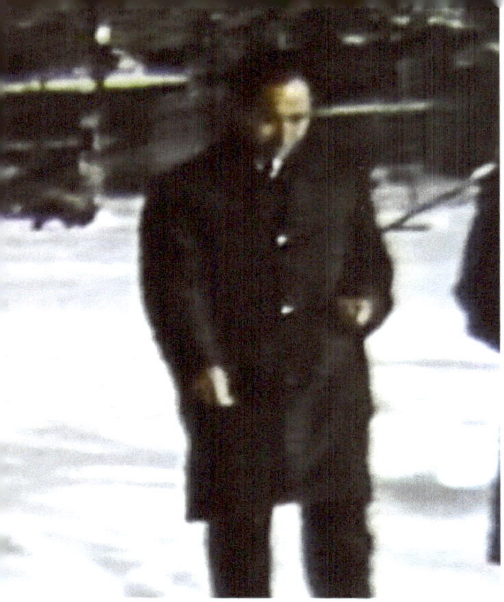
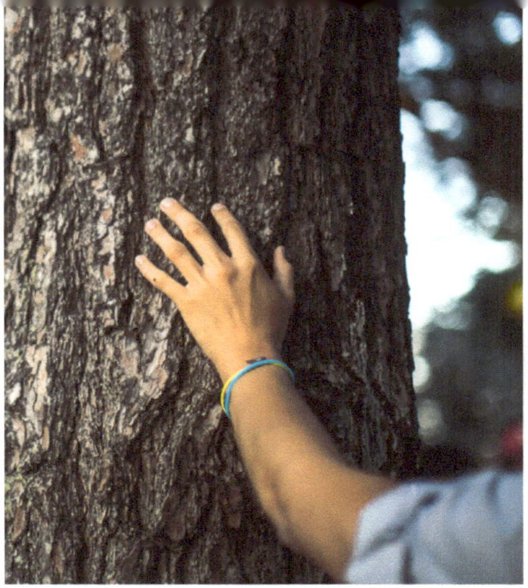
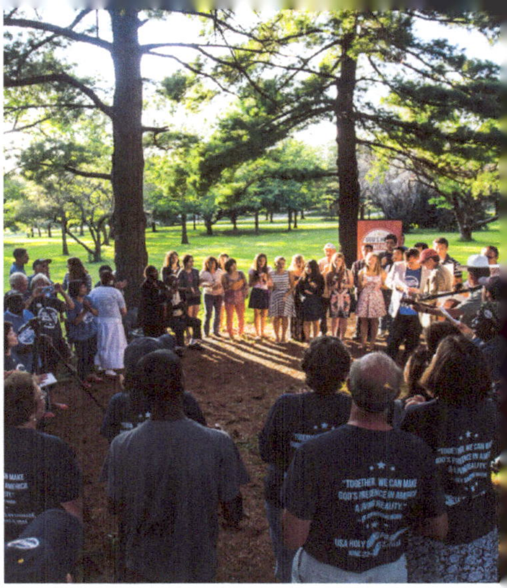
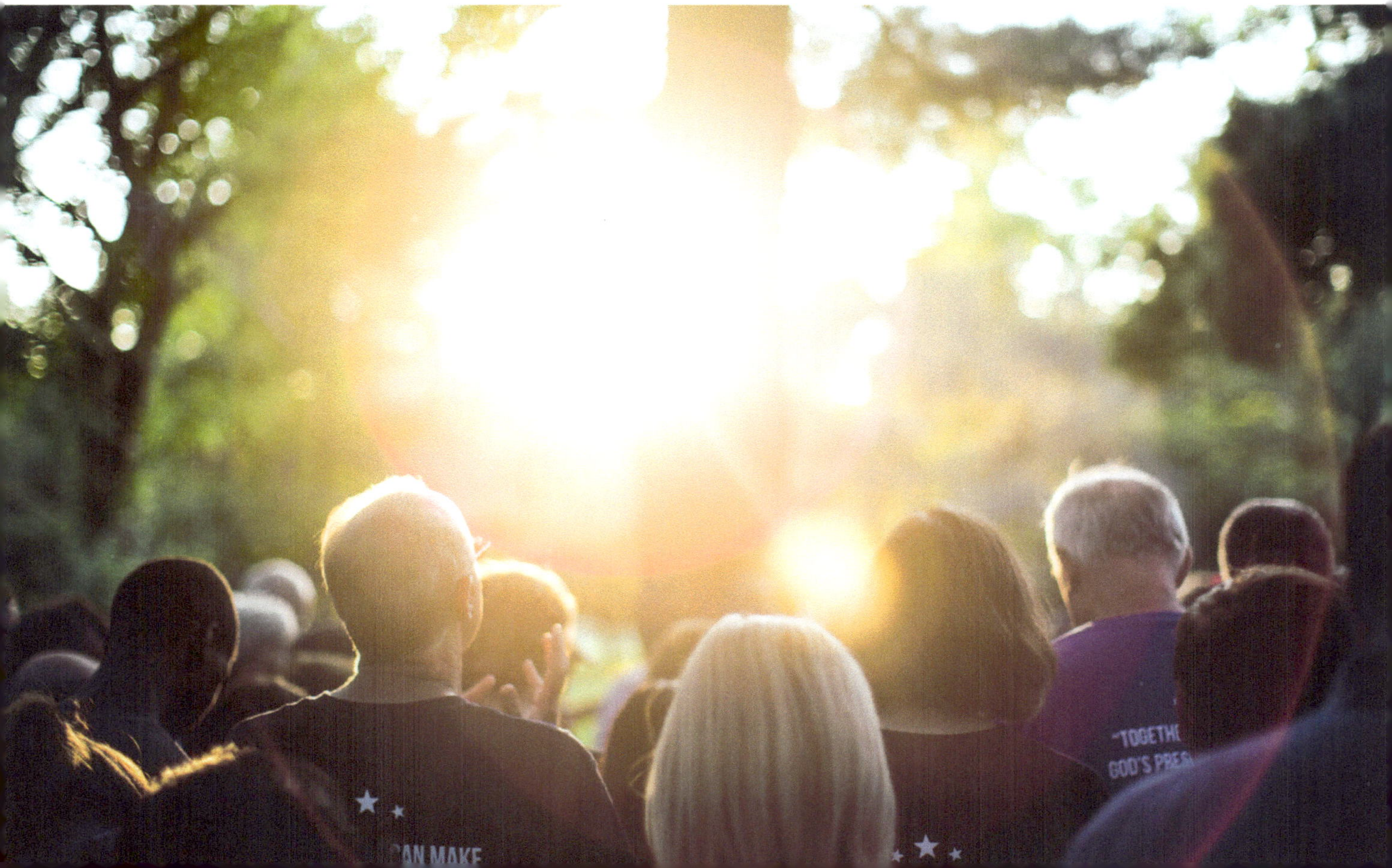

CHEYENNE, WYOMING

HOLY GROUND ⭐ 48

EST: MARCH 24, 1965
GPS COORDINATES: 41°09'22.5"N 104°49'51.0"W

LIONS PARK
4603 Lions Park Dr.,
Cheyenne WY 82001

LOCATION

The Cheyenne Holy Ground was initially in Holiday Park but is now gone due to construction. The re-dedicated Holy Ground is in Lions Park. It is marked by the second-to-last fir tree by a stone monument in the southeast section of the park next to a line of trees.

JOURNAL ENTRY

The road to Wyoming was also icy, and once again they prayed unceasingly that they wouldn't skid off the road. Very few drivers were even attempting travel that day, and they passed abandoned cars all along the way. Yet they continued on. Neither snow nor rain nor sleet nor hail. ... Rev. Moon blessed a Holy Ground in Lions Park in Cheyenne, Wyoming, with a toy railroad track running beside it.

To Mrs. Moon

I believe that you understand well that I am always yearning for you, the precious True Mother who is centered on the Will. Whether we die or live, we must overcome many things to carry out the Will.

-Rev. Moon, March 25, 1965, Denver, CO

GOD'S HOPE for AMERICA.org
55 HOLY GROUNDS ★ 43 DAYS ★ JUNE 22–AUGUST 3, 2014

49 CHEYENNE, WY
JULY 30, 2014

DENVER, COLORADO

HOLY GROUND ⭐ 49

EST: MARCH 25, 1965
GPS COORDINATES: 39°44'43.2"N 104°57'26.7"W

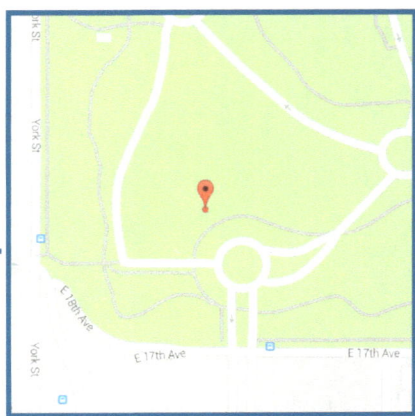

CITY PARK
E. 17th Ave. and
City Park Esplanade
Denver, CO 80206

LOCATION

The Denver Holy Ground is in City Park. It is located in a sports field near a large statue on the south side of the park. A large elm tree was originally in the field but has since been cut down. This area still marks the Holy Ground.

JOURNAL ENTRY

The party drove in several cars to City Park in Denver, Colorado, where Rev. Moon chose a very large tree as the center of the Holy Ground. Rev. Moon led the way through about 6 inches of snow on the ground, with everyone following the path that he had made. "We'll leave early," Rev. Moon said. "Right after we bless the Holy Ground." After blessing the Holy Ground, they went to the State Capitol, where Rev. Moon took some earth and a stone. On their way again, the car suddenly rebelled. By the time it could be repaired, it was 3:30 in the afternoon. Precious time had been lost.

To Mrs. Moon

Night has passed, and today is March 25th. In three days, it will already be two months since we parted. ... Today, I write to you from Denver, the state capital of Colorado. When you see this letter, you will probably search for Denver on a map. After breakfast, I will drive to Salt Lake City.

-Rev. Moon, March 25, 1965, Denver, CO

SALT LAKE CITY, UTAH

HOLY GROUND ⭐ 50

EST: MARCH 26, 1965
GPS COORDINATES: 40°43'29.5"N 111°51'01.4"W

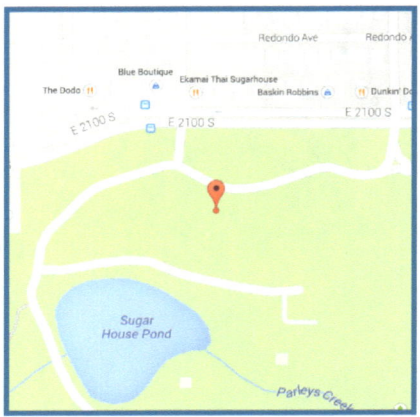

BIG FIELD PAVILION, SUGARHOUSE PARK
Near 2100 S 1500 E., Salt Lake City, UT 84106

LOCATION

Atop a hill high above the capital, overlooking Salt Lake Valley and the greenest of green fields and majestic blue mountains, is the Salt Lake City Holy Ground in Ensign Park. It is located on top of Ensign Park Peak, a small mountain off of North Churchill Dr., a cul-de-sac surrounded by houses.

JOURNAL ENTRY

Well after dark, they arrived in Salt Lake City, Utah. The next morning they took a quick tour of the Mormon Tabernacle, a grand church built by the Mormons in the city they had founded. Rev. Moon blessed a Holy Ground on a bald mountaintop nearby. The view of the city on one side and the snow-covered mountains on the other provided a stunning setting. As usual, they couldn't take much time to enjoy its beauty. "Kapshida! [Let's go!]" Rev. Moon said.

To Mrs. Moon

I am concerned about you in your condition [with child] making effort every morning to go to the Holy Ground. But on the other hand, I think it is such a beautiful thing that you are doing.

-Rev. Moon, March 25, 1965, Denver, CO

BOISE, IDAHO

HOLY GROUND 51

EST: MARCH 26, 1965
GPS COORDINATES: 43°36'28.3"N 116°12'14.9"W

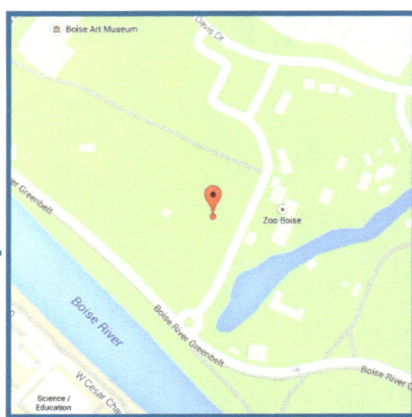

JULIA DAVIS PARK
355 Julia Davis Dr.,
Boise, ID 83702

LOCATION

The Boise Holy Ground is located in Julia Davis Park. It is located near the entrance to the Boise Zoo. The Holy Ground is marked by a large tree at the far end of a picnic shelter past the zoo entrance.

JOURNAL ENTRY

They headed for Boise, Idaho, and went to Julia Davis Park to bless the Holy Ground. As the rain softly fell, Rev. Moon chose a spot to bless a Holy Ground. Then, "Kapshida!" And they were off again.

FINAL WORDS

American brothers and sisters should not have an interest only in America or pray just for America. ... You must not shed tears just for America. ... you must shed them for the sake of the world. You must stand in the position of loving America because you love the world.

-Reverend Sun Myung Moon

MISSOULA, MONTANA

HOLY GROUND

EST: MARCH 27, 1965
GPS COORDINATES: 46°52'30.8"N 113°58'50.2"W

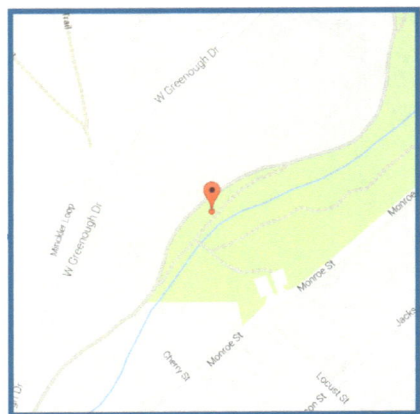

LOCATION

The Missoula Holy Ground is located in Greenough Park next to a clear, bubbling river called Rattlesnake Creek. It is at the south end of the park near a group of evergreen trees, northwest of a bridge crossing the creek. The Holy Ground is marked by a central tree with another small tree to its left.

GREENOUGH PARK
1000 Monroe St.,
Missoula, MT 59802

JOURNAL ENTRY

Interstate 15 in Idaho is known as the "scenic route." Scenic routes are not generally the fastest way to one's destination, and Interstate 15 was no exception. The road curved around, under and over hill and dale, mountain and valley. Often the car would slide a little way along the ice-slick roads before responding to the promptings of its driver. The view was breathtaking! In Missoula, Rev. Moon blessed a Holy Ground surrounded by pine and fir trees and lofty, smooth mountains. The rushing waters of a brook nearby accompanied his words.

FINAL WORDS

Before there were Americans, God was America's owner. Even before there were Native Americans, God was the owner of America. Therefore, the people God loves the most will become the owners of America.

-Reverend Sun Myung Moon

SEATTLE, WASHINGTON

HOLY GROUND ⭐ 53

EST: MARCH 28, 1965
GPS COORDINATES: 47°33'04.6"N 122°14'58.8"W

SEWARD PARK
5902 Lake Washington Blvd. S.,
Seattle, WA 98118

LOCATION

The Seattle Holy Ground is located in Seward Park, on the edge of Lake Washington. It is three-quarters of a mile past the park entrance, near two picnic shelters. A small path in the woods across the road from the first picnic pavilion, leads to a large tree just before a meadow which marks the Holy Ground.

JOURNAL ENTRY

The road conditions from Missoula, Montana, to Spokane, Washington, forced them to put chains on the tires, and they inched over the mountain passes with catlike precision. Finally, from Spokane to Seattle, they were able to soar through the crisp night air, slowing only for the Cascade Range, and reached their destination around 4 a.m. on March 28. After a few hours' sleep they headed to the Holy Ground in a park overlooking Lake Washington, they drove on to St. Helens, Oregon.

FINAL WORDS

American citizens must understand that God gave America boundless blessings for 200 years. ... God helped America gain a larger population than that of its enemies. He gave America blessings that would help the country overcome materialism. America is responsible for the strength of the right side, and no matter what occurs she must defend God and Christianity until the very end.

-Reverend Sun Myung Moon

On our way to Seattle, the bus stopped at the breathtaking cascades of Snoqualmie Falls in Washington State. Tour participants scattered around the park taking pictures of the falls and talking with fellow visitors.

PORTLAND, OREGON

HOLY GROUND 54

EST: MARCH 29, 1965

GPS COORDINATES: 45°30'46.2"N 122°35'34.5"W

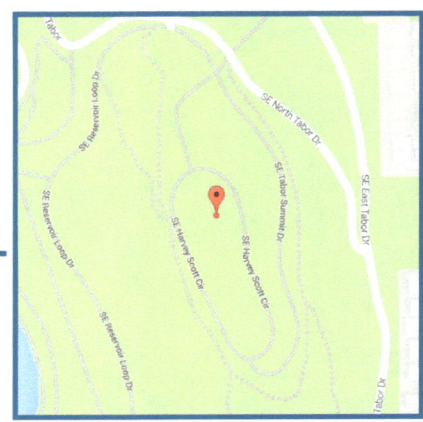

MOUNT TABOR PARK
S.E. Salmon Street,
Portland, OR 97215

LOCATION

The Portland Holy Ground is located in Mount Tabor City Park, atop Mount Tabor Park. The site is marked by a grove of large evergreen trees. The Holy Ground is between three of these trees, signifying a trinity. It is located on the east side of the summit.

JOURNAL ENTRY

Spring greeted them on the West Coast. After dinner in St. Helens, Oregon, they proceeded on to Portland. After a night's rest, Rev. Moon gave his final official blessing to the United States on March 29 at Mount Tabor Park in Portland, overlooking the city. Rev. Moon chose a large tree, which was actually three trees in one, as the site of the Holy Ground. When he was finished, he looked to the darkening sky and said quietly with great emotion, "Heavenly Father, it is fulfilled." All 48 states on the mainland had received their Holy Grounds.

FINAL WORDS

In total, I established 55 Holy Grounds in America. Today, there is no one protecting these Holy Grounds. The Unification Church is not developing because no one is taking care of the Holy Grounds.

-Reverend Sun Myung Moon

EUGENE, OREGON

HOLY GROUND ⭐ 55

EST: MARCH 29, 1965
GPS COORDINATES: 44°02'19.6"N 123°03'29.5"W

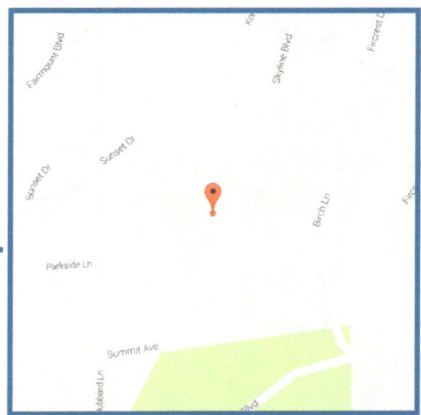

HENDRICKS PARK
2198 Summit Ave,
Eugene, OR 97403

LOCATION

On day 43 the God's Hope for America tour reached its final destination: Eugene, Oregon. The park where the Holy Ground is situated does not allow loud public gatherings. The group gathered in meditative prayer as they tearfully celebrated the completion of this historic event.

JOURNAL ENTRY

We journeyed to Eugene, Oregon, birthplace of our American Family. To reward this historic city, Rev. Moon blessed one more Holy Ground, the 55th in America. This time, when it was completed, Rev. Moon raised his hands in a strong gesture of victory and shouted in English, "Finished!" He strode away like a victor. Everyone strode victoriously after him. After a well-deserved victory feast, they headed on down the highway to San Francisco, where the circle would be complete.

FINAL WORDS

All of you Americans here today must understand clearly how many hardships God experienced and how much He suffered so He could prepare to give this land such a huge blessing. An incredible teaching must be born in this land ... a teaching that exists for the entire world. One world family must be established here.

-Reverend Sun Myung Moon

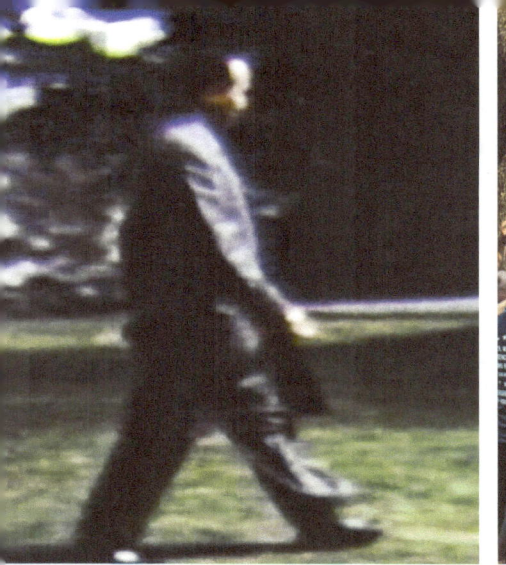

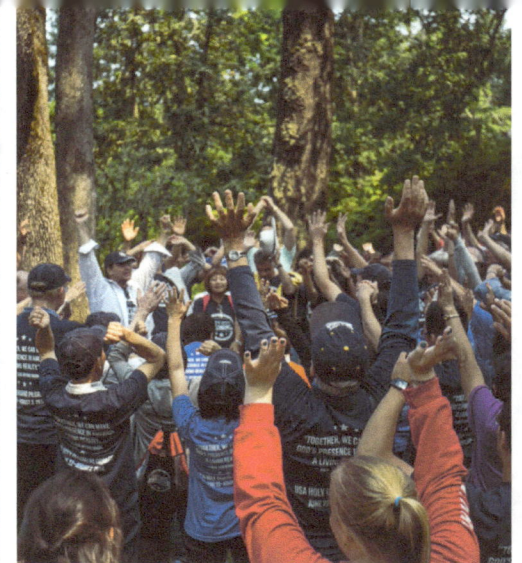

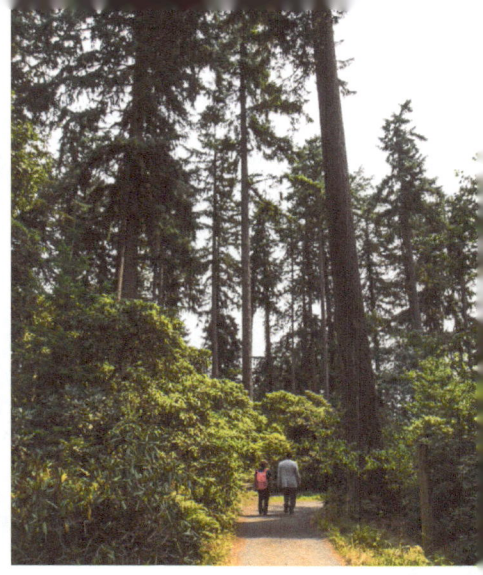

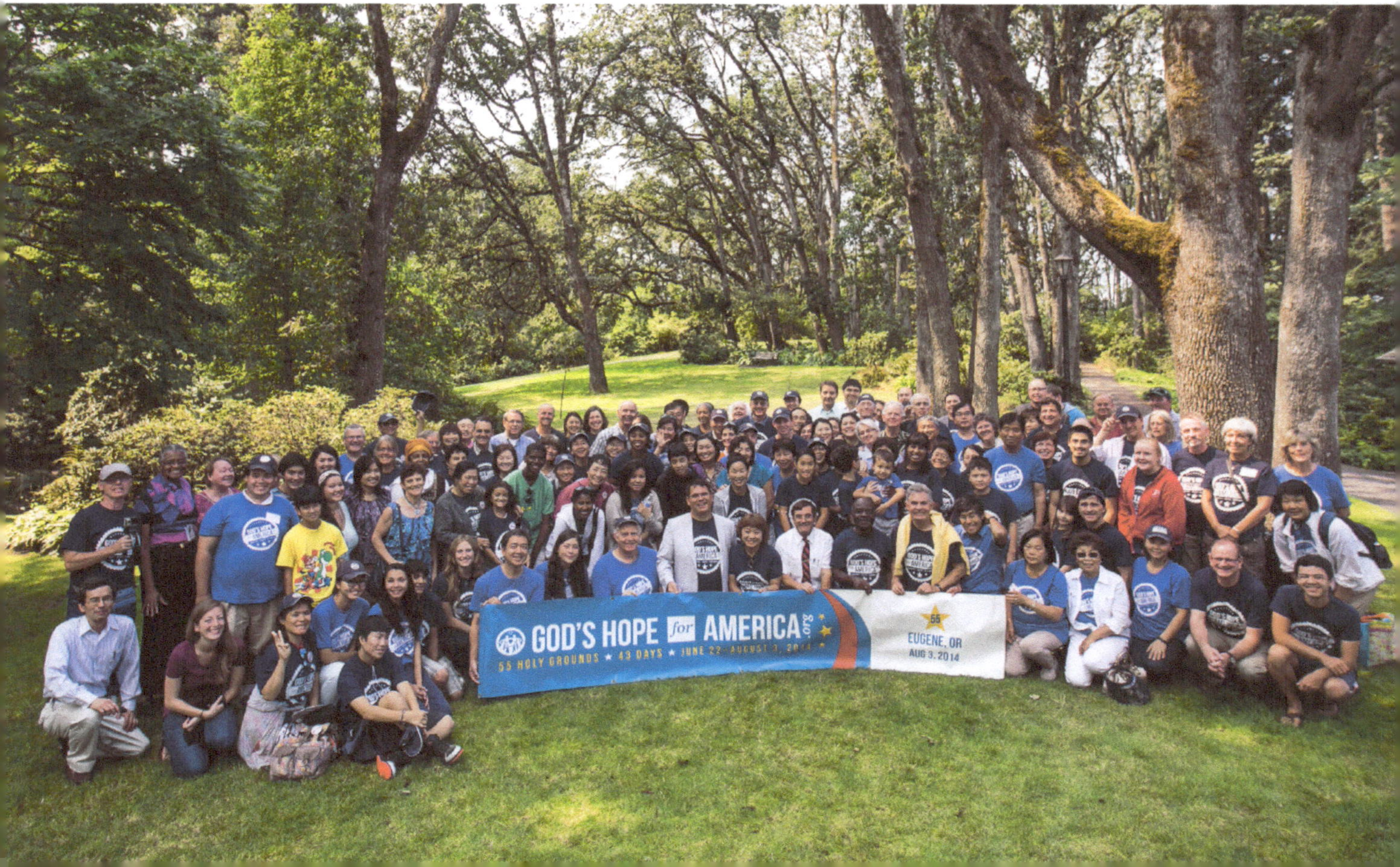
GOD'S HOPE for AMERICA.org
55 HOLY GROUNDS ★ 43 DAYS ★ JUNE 22–AUGUST 3, 2014
55
EUGENE, OR
AUG 3. 2014

RICA.org

DID YOU KNOW THAT ON THE TOUR...

rode on the buses

meals eaten

miles traveled

hotel rooms

holy ground attendees

bookmarks

postcards

caps

bumper stickers

swag bags

maps

pens

stickers

tshirts

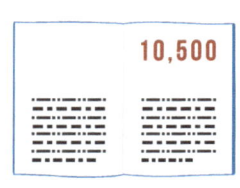
speech booklets

go pro photos
(camera mounted on the bus front window)

GOD'S HOPE FOR AMERICA
Roles and Responsibilities

Adresses and GPS Coordinates

We have taken great care to list addresses accurately. Often the address is a local park, or place you can park close to the actual Holy Ground itself. The GPS coordinates in this book represent the Holy Grounds themselves.

While you could use just the GPS, we recommend working with the local pastor to accurately locate the Holy Ground site.

Executive Committee

Dr. Ki Hoon Kim
Dr. Michael Balcomb
Dr. Chang Shik Yang
Rev. David Rendel

Pastors

Ernest Patton
Manoj Jacob
Gary Chidester
Kazuo Takami
John Jackson
Kevin Thompson
Andrew Compton
Mark Beaudoin
Garrun and Yusun Abrahams
Rosemary Yokoi
David Roberts
George Kazakos

Affiliated Organizations

Tom Cutts, American Clergy Leadership Conference
Crescentia DeGoede, Blessing and Family Ministry
Hiroshi and Hatsune Inose, Kodan
Angelika Selle, Women's Federation for World Peace USA
Ricardo de Sena, Universal Peace Federation USA
Naokimi Ushiroda, Collegiate Assoc. for the Research of Principles

Operations / Logistics / Legal

David Rendel
Luke Higuchi
Olga Majitova
Hiroshi Suzuki
Kaye Allen
Thanh Lee
Louis Perlowitz
Tal Zorer

Accounting and Financial Affairs

Michael Jenkins
Chohei Shimizu
Asae Sattinger

Marketing and Outreach

Demian Dunkley
Nocynthia Shibuya

Driver

Paul Vetterli, Badger Coaches

Photo / Video

Toshi Tagawa
Koichi Nakai
Riky Johnson
Graeme Carmichael

Web Development

Sean Kim
Gerry Servito
Daniel Castillo

Design

Jonathan Gullery
Young Heller
LeeHee Wolf
Abigail Zambon
Judilee King

Editorial

Shinyoung Chang
Kimera Wachna
Jeanne Castillo
Dr. Michael Balcomb

AFTERWORD

So What Is God's Hope for America?

Now, 43 days later, we've reached the end! From San Francisco through the southern states, up the East Coast and back to Oregon, it has been a tremendous journey of profound realizations, devoted prayer, joyous reunions and enthusiastic responses from the people we met. One of the most common things we heard on the road, by people seeing the large "God's Hope for America" banner along the side of the bus, was, "Now, this is what we need!"

We have visited 55 Holy Grounds, in 48 states, in 43 days, but God's Hope for America doesn't end here, just as Father Moon only just began his mission in America with establishing the Holy Grounds. His footsteps continue, and we will continue to follow them and carry his vision. This pilgrimage is a burst of momentum to power us forward and align America and the world with God's Kingdom. We've paved the way for future pilgrimages as well; consider taking your own pilgrimage with your family, friends or your youth group to each Holy Ground, or to a few in your region.

Our united and continuous prayer will stand strong and represent God's voice across the nation. It's time to spread God's hope to our neighbors, our coworkers, and new people we've just met. There are so many people out there who are ready to meet God or to dedicate their lives to building what Father and Mother Moon have envisioned and worked so hard to build. We hope you can look back at the highlights of the trip and gain new inspiration whenever you need it.

Before you go, think about this: How are YOU God's Hope for America?

www.ingramcontent.com/pod-product-compliance
Lightning Source LLC
Chambersburg PA
CBHW050736110526
44591CB00003B/39